HSC
Health & Safety Commission
Railways Industry Advisory Committee

PREVENTION OF TRESPASS AND VANDALISM ON RAILWAYS

A GOOD PRACTICE GUIDE

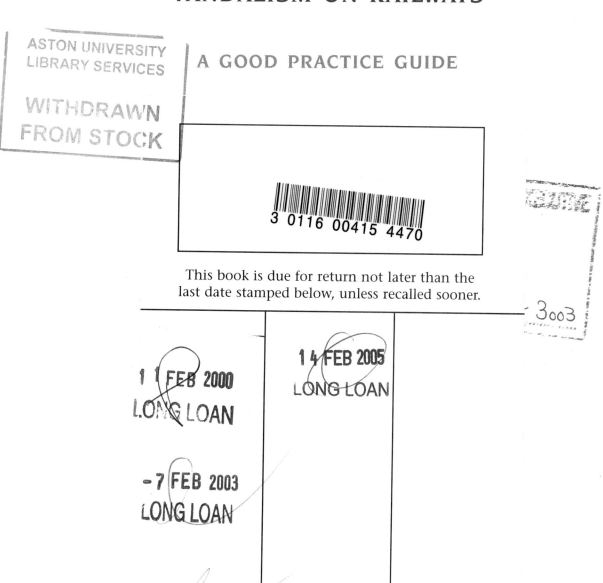

HSE BOOKS

CONTENTS

Case studies

1 Railtrack/South West Trains/English, Welsh and Scottish Rail/ AMEC Rail/British Transport Police

Case studies

2 Railtrack Southern Zone

3 Railtrack Scotland Loss Control Group remit

4 Midland Main Line

Case studies

5 Railtrack

6 Railtrack South Zone

7 London Underground Ltd

8 Cardiff Railway Company CCTV trial at Treforrest railway station

9 Connex South Central

10 Railtrack

11 Thameslink

Case studies

12 Connex South Eastern

13 Thameslink/British Transport Police

14 Mercy Travel Limited (MTL) security and audit

15 Operation Scarecrow

Foreword

I am pleased to introduce this publication, which has been produced by the Railway Industry Advisory Committee (RIAC). It is intended to provide the railway industry and other interested bodies with practical help in combating trespass on, and vandalism to, railway stations, trains, infrastructure and equipment. These problems are still on the increase, despite the best efforts of the railway industry and others. The 1998/99 Railway Group Safety Plan recognises the scale and growth of the problem, and the industry has agreed to do more to combat it. Other railway operators have also formulated strategies to combat the problem. I hope this guidance will help the industry by focusing on measures with a proven track record.

Trespass and vandalism are related, but there are also distinct differences between them. Most trespass is not malicious and puts the trespassers themselves in danger. Vandalism is malicious and endangers other people. The case studies which form the core of this book show that it is often useful to differentiate between them when developing effective control measures.

Suicides and suspected suicides represent a particularly tragic element of trespass, and one that is extremely difficult to tackle. Taking action to reduce the frequency of these incidents benefits the industry and society as a whole, as well as the individuals concerned. I am pleased to see that the railway industry is addressing the issue separately.

Trespass and vandalism also affect how passengers view the security – or otherwise – of rail travel. This book also looks at how general security control can be improved. The Commission welcomes the Department of Environment, Transport and the Regions' Secure Stations scheme and the Association of Train Operators' Code of Practice for passenger security.

I recommend this book to everyone interested in improving the safety and security of the railways and encouraging greater use of the rail network. I am convinced that there is a sound business case for tackling this problem and I would expect all railway companies to have a policy and strategy for prevention. Better reporting of incidents will help everyone to refine their business cases for action, and all efforts and actions should be properly evaluated.

The Health and Safety Commission (HSC) and RIAC will continue to play a positive role in supporting the efforts of the industry to combat and reduce trespass and vandalism. It is a task that is vital both to the industry and to society.

Frank J Davies, CBE, OStJ
Chairman, Health and Safety Commission

KEY POINTS AND SUGGESTED ACTIONS

Key points in this section are the need to develop a coherent policy on preventing trespass and vandalism. Such a policy should be based on developing an evaluation process, sharing information and co-ordinating activities between all parties involved.

This book demonstrates the considerable commitment and energy of the railway industry in its efforts to combat the many problems of trespass and vandalism. There are many more initiatives which have not been specifically referred to or illustrated.

Putting the book together has brought to light a number of general points which could improve the effectiveness of existing activities. These are as follows.

Management issues

Analysis and evaluation

There are many preventative initiatives focusing on the main problem areas. It is difficult to tell whether these initiatives are effective or not as so little evaluation is carried out.

Suggested action: an industry-wide evaluation process should be developed

Reporting processes

Reports of incidents are often assembled in different forms by different organisations within the industry. This means there is little common referencing, reporting or statistics.

Suggested action: a reporting process should be developed so that reports of incidents are shared by the interested parties and can be cross-referenced

Cost assessment

The total cost of trespass and vandalism has never been properly assessed. This makes it difficult to justify the cost of remedial measures. Assessing the cost of minutes lost has helped to focus activity but this is only one element of the total cost. In cases where comprehensive data has been available (in Case Study 1 and the SAFE initiative in South Yorkshire), it was useful in justifying remedial measures.

Suggested action: information on all trespass and vandalism-related costs should be shared across the industry

Policies and strategies

There are many instances of organisations developing policies and strategies individually but few examples of co-operation with other organisations. On occasions when a collective effort has been made, it has not always been successful.

Suggested action: collective policies and strategies should be developed throughout the industry. Railtrack should take the lead on Railtrack controlled infrastructure; in most other cases the operator should take the lead. Public transport strategies such as South Yorkshire's SAFE initiative may be appropriate for other areas, particularly large conurbations

Resources and structures

The provision of management, resources and the organisational structures set up to develop and direct initiatives varies quite widely across the industry. Improved focus could increase effectiveness in a number of cases.

Suggested action: all organisations should review their resources and structures to make sure they are addressing trespass and vandalism problems effectively

Other points to note

The case studies suggest that most problems are best tackled by a combination of actions rather than a single activity. This is especially true where there are persistent and endemic problems of vandalism.

A lot of vandalism occurs in areas of social deprivation, where behavioural problems affect the whole community. In these circumstances, it would be beneficial to work with organisations which address more general social problems.

Most initiatives aimed at young people have focused on school visits. While school visits are unlikely to influence the behaviour of current perpetrators, they may well have an effect on the future behaviour of other children.

Very few activities are aimed at influencing the age group responsible for most trespass and vandalism issues. We need to direct more effort into reaching these young people.

Graffiti and litter on railway property create a bad impression. We need to increase our efforts to prevent and control these problems.

Line-side materials and redundant structures seem to encourage trespass and vandalism. Railways would benefit from removing these materials and structures.

We could not find any instances of activities aimed at preventing reoffending and discouraging other potential vandals or trespassers. We should consider ways in which this could be addressed.

1 – INTRODUCTION

It is important to address the issue of trespass and vandalism and to frame appropriate responses through a better understanding of the problem. This publication aims to spread good practice based on actions and initiatives which are already taking place and to look at the lessons to be learnt from them.

Setting the scene

1 The overall safety record on the railways continues to improve. London Underground and the former British Rail adopted a tighter focus on safety management, which has been sustained by the privatised industry. This has been a major factor behind the improvement. Similar efforts by other operators have also brought about improvements. However, one area that shows no sign of improvement is that of trespass and vandalism. In fact, it may even be getting worse.

2 In 1996/97, when the number of railway fatalities (25) was the lowest on record, 133 people were killed as a result of trespassing on to railway property. Of these, 10 were children aged 15 or under. This is a 27% increase on the 107 trespassers who were killed in 1995/96. There was a further 10% increase in all such fatalities in 1997/98 including a further 122 people killed on the railway and recorded as suicides. Figure 1 shows the numbers over the last 20 years. They represent a major human tragedy and a substantial cost to the industry.

3 Equally alarming, although fortunately without the same fatal outcomes, is the number of train accidents caused by vandalism and other malicious acts. In 1996/97, vandalism and other malicious acts caused 51% of all train accidents. In 1997/98 this proportion increased to about 60%. Of the 302 fires on trains in 1996/97, 171 (56%) were started deliberately. In 1997/98, the figures were 344 and 206 (60%). Figures 2 and 3 show that the number of train accidents due to malicious action and the number of fires on trains started deliberately have risen in recent years. While the number of fatalities and

Figure 1 – Fatalities to Trespassers 1976–1997/98

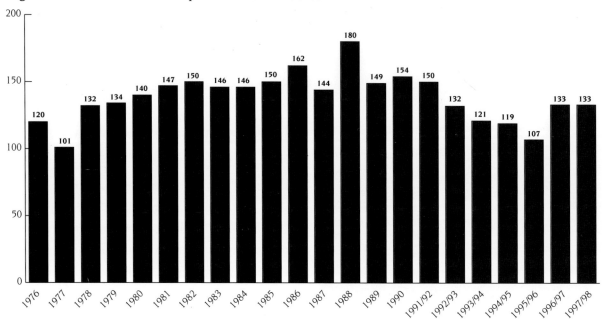

Figure 2 – Train accidents due to malicious action 1976–1997/98

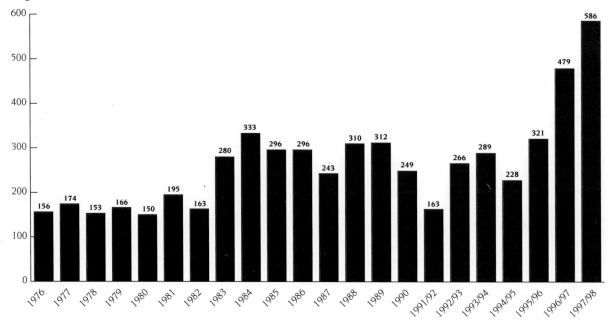

Data for 96/97, 97/98 excludes malicious acts of damage to drivers' windscreens

injuries arising from those malicious acts has been low, the potential for a major accident or incident is always there.

4 Instances of vandalism, damage to railway property and equipment are an ongoing problem, although they are not reported consistently. Graffiti on trains, buildings and structures also gives railway customers a sense of insecurity.

5 The effect of vandalism on passengers and railway staff should always be borne in mind. Exposure to incidents can create concern and even trauma in the people concerned. It results both in reduced use of

Case study 1 – Railtrack/ South West Trains/English, Welsh and Scottish Rail/AMEC Rail/British Transport Police

Objective

To reduce acts of vandalism and trespass on the railway line in the Bedfont area.

Dates
July 1997.

Background

The area concerned is an 800m stretch of line from Feltham station towards Bedfont. There is a housing estate near the railway line where a path leads alongside the railway through some general waste ground to a footbridge and then to the local school. There is also a small gully beside the railway fence which gives people standing on the waste ground the impression that they are level with the railway line. It is not possible to see the fence from the waste ground.

A wide range of offences were being committed in the area:

- trespass — the railway being used for short cuts;
- vandalism/trespass — objects frequently placed on the line;
- vandalism — objects thrown at trains from an adjacent footpath;
- vandalism — objects thrown onto the line or at trains from footbridge;
- vandalism — objects thrown at trains from a large mound of waste earth adjacent to bridge;
- vandalism — objects thrown across railway damaging adjacent housing scheme;
- vandalism — objects thrown at Eastleigh at freight service (transit vans);
- vandalism — vehicles driven into boundary fence;
- vandalism — constant incidents of arson on railway embankment.

The problem

Poor fencing and footbridge caging offer easy access to the railway line. The route to the school passes beside and over the railway line, allowing children to trespass and throw stones. The police also believed a drug dealer was working out of a house on the estate and that buyers were taking a short cut straight across the railway lines.

The solution

Waterloo Area Train Services Delivery Manager (TSDM) and his group developed the following initiatives.

The cost

The group worked with South West Trains (SWT), English Welsh and Scottish (EWS) and AMEC Rail to calculate the annual cost of the incidents. The cost included delays to trains, damage to rolling stock, repairs to rolling stock, damage to infrastructure and damage to vehicles in transit. The final sum was £300 000 per year. The most serious concern was safety, as passengers on trains had been injured by objects striking trains.

Immediate actions

The scale of the problem required urgent action to reduce the number of incidents. Incident data was analysed to identify the times and types of incidents. A trespass and vandalism group set up at Feltham included delegates from the British Transport Police (BTP). Actions taken included:

- high-profile visits to the area at critical times by both Railtrack and BTP;
- a leaflet drop to local residents asking for help in reporting and identifying offenders;
- contacting Hounslow Council to discuss the environment beyond the railway boundary;
- more school visits in the Feltham area to raise awareness of dangers;
- contacting building contractors about working together to set up a CCTV scheme.

These actions reduced the number of incidents and gave the group time to come up with more permanent measures to eliminate the problem.

The wide range of offences being committed meant the group had to come up with different measures for different problems:

- trespass – a palisade fence was installed alongside the existing fence to provide a double obstacle;
- vandalism – a joint Railtrack/Hounslow Council project completely caged both the ramps and span of bridge;
- the Council removed the waste mound of earth;
- a screen fence was erected inside the existing boundary fence so no objects could be thrown directly at or into the path of a train;
- signs warning people about the 24-hour CCTV surveillance were attached to a 100m stretch of fencing;
- wooden panel fencing alongside the boundary fence for the housing estate was removed;
- high-profile visits continued during school holidays. The newly formed Trespass & Vandalism Hit Squad visited the area frequently;
- AMEC inspected the area regularly and made immediate repairs to damaged fencing.

The outcome

Since the projects were completed in July 1997, there has been some vandalism to parts of the fence. It has been dealt with swiftly and the incidents are decreasing. There have been no recorded incidents of trespass and vandalism since July 1997.

2 – MANAGEMENT SYSTEMS AND PROCESSES

To effectively combat trespass and vandalism, an organisation needs to develop a clear policy and put coherent systems in place.

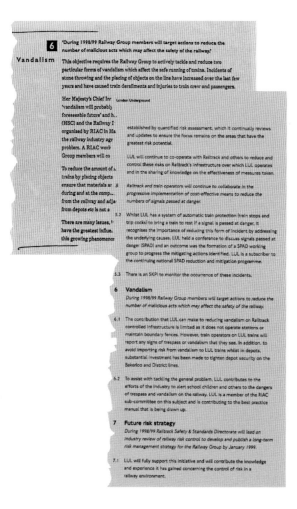

22 Effective management arrangements are critical in any issue affecting a company or industry. This is especially important in relation to trespass and vandalism, which have many manifestations. The restructuring of the railway industry has led to an increased emphasis on the separation of responsibilities and management structures and on contractual relationships. This means that a clear definition of responsibilities and co-operative management arrangements are even more important.

Policy statement

23 A clear statement of policy is a vital starting point and can map out the direction of any activity. Making measures to control trespass and vandalism a specific objective in the Railway Group and London Underground Safety Plans for 1998/99 is thus an important step. It is essential to incorporate specific plans for tackling trespass and vandalism in the safety plan objectives of individual companies in the Railway Group. Railtrack might also usefully include plans for trespass and vandalism in its Network Management Statement.

24 Train operators' railway safety cases require them to produce a safety policy statement, which is subject to annual review. A number of operators make specific reference to controlling trespass and vandalism. Other operators could benefit from doing the same. Some infrastructure contractors have specific policy statements on trespass and vandalism and this practice should be extended.

Organisation

25 Every organisation needs to establish clear and specific responsibility for dealing with trespass and vandalism issues. Responsibility for addressing trespass and vandalism varies widely across the many railway companies. Tackling these issues should form part of a manager's job description.

26 The manager responsible for this area needs to be supported in two ways. Managers need clear access to the managing director as well as to a group of colleagues who can provide direction and support. This group can take a variety of forms, and might form part of a general safety management meeting. It is important that trespass and vandalism is a specific element of the group's terms of reference. A representative from the public affairs section should be included to make sure the external aspects of managing trespass and vandalism are not neglected.

Co-operation

27 Controlling trespass and vandalism is an industry-wide issue. A forum for industry operators would help focus and co-ordinate activities and resources. Again, this can be included in a general safety/loss control agenda, as shown by Railtrack Scotland. Some operators, like Railtrack South Zone (Case study 2) have a specific forum. Any such forum should consider station and line-side problems, and maintenance and renewal contractors should be involved. Discussions on station issues could involve other train operators and anyone who stands to benefit directly. Just as a policy statement is an important starting point for individual operators, it can also be a useful tool for regulating cross-industry activities. The trespass and vandalism charter initiated by Railtrack Great Western is a useful example (see Case study 2).

28 Any formal environmental policy should also refer to the environmental aspects of trespass and vandalism.

29 Vandalism is a problem for all forms of public transport. In South Yorkshire a combined approach by rail and bus operators, police forces and the Passenger Transport Executive has resulted in the SAFE (Supporting a Friendly Environment) strategy, which addresses common issues. The emphasis in the recent White Paper on integrated transport on co-operation between public transport operators suggests that this approach might be usefully applied elsewhere.

Planning

30 Effective action and deployment of resources requires careful analysis and planning of any actions. Cardiff Railways has a computer-based analysis system enabling them to focus on priority locations. The crime pattern analysis facilities of BTP and other police forces can help identify 'black spots' where action should be concentrated. Co-ordination between operators and the police will result in more effective use of resources.

31 Operators – especially those who have interfaces with several area zones or management units of different organisations – have stressed the importance of a consistent policy and application throughout the network. This applies to all sections of the industry. The benefits of developing a uniform approach are clear but will be greater if scope remains for adapting any proposals to local circumstances.

Review

32 It is equally important to review the effectiveness of actions and initiatives. It is tempting for managers to move on to the next priority once action has been taken, without assessing how beneficial that action has been.

33 Those planning engineering activities need to minimise risks by taking into account the implications of trespass and vandalism. The physical security of access points and material before work and the removal of materials and equipment at the end are important considerations which may also have commercial benefits.

Involving staff

34 Staff attitudes have an important role to play in controlling trespass and vandalism. Staff need to be motivated to report all instances of trespass and vandalism, however minor. There should be simple and speedy procedures for reporting all incidents immediately. Management have a major responsibility to make sure this happens.

35 To achieve widespread reporting, staff need to understand the nature of the problem and the part that they can play in addressing it. This means clear and regular two-way communication, including feedback on progress and in particular on the use made of reports submitted by staff. A personal response to any staff member reporting an instance will help to reinforce commitment.

36 Employees often need convincing about management commitment to addressing problems of trespass and vandalism. Any changes in practice, particularly withdrawal from an initiative or programme, should be explained carefully to reduce negative reaction and to encourage active employee support.

Case study 2 – Railtrack Southern Zone

Background

Since April 1994, Public Affairs have taken the lead in managing trespass and vandalism on Railtrack Southern Zone but incidents continued to increase. In January 1997, the Production Strategy Manager volunteered to manage trespass and vandalism and take over as zone champion, with an emphasis on 'doing something' about the problem.

The process

At a joint meeting in January 1997, Southern Zone customers and suppliers helped to develop a management process to manage trespass and vandalism. The meeting resulted in Railtrack forming a steering group to support local multi-industry groups based on our four production areas. The remits for both groups emphasised that the local groups would be the 'doers'.

The steering group would support the local trespass and vandalism groups by helping to clear any obstacles in their way, offering help with funding and business cases and generally spreading best practice.

Steering group

The steering group is chaired by the Production Strategy Manager and consists of the four area TSDMs, Public Affairs and BTP. The trains safety and standards managers from Connex South Eastern, South Central and South West were subsequently invited to join the group so that their senior managers would know about initiatives at local levels.

Local groups

The area TSDMs chaired these, with the local Train Operating Company (TOC) Manager, suppliers and BTP.

Results

At the end of 1997/98, 69 695 delay minutes were attributed to trespass and vandalism. This was 11.7% down on the 1996/97 figure of 82 392 delay minutes.

Trespass and vandalism – steering group

Purpose

The steering group will strategically manage the zone's response to trespass and vandalism issues.

Terms of reference

■ Identify areas with significant trespass and vandalism problems and give local groups a remit to make a full review and put forward recommendations.

■ Endorse or reject the conclusions and recommendations of local trespass and vandalism groups which will analyse trends in trespass and vandalism incidents.

■ Co-ordinate the output of local trespass and vandalism groups, promoting best practice where appropriate.

- Review recommendations of local groups and ensure that cost-effective solutions are produced to reduce the number of trespass and vandalism incidents and their effect on the zone's business.

- Where necessary, ensure that business cases are submitted at the appropriate level to fund initiatives.

- Develop and evaluate new possibilities for enhanced security on Railtrack's property, considering both physical and other approaches.

- Develop greater awareness among all people employed in the zone (whether by Railtrack, its contractors or customers) of the importance of prompt reporting of trespass. Staff also need to be aware of situations where trespass and vandalism could occur and should report these too.

- Co-ordinate the school visits programmes across the zone.

- Review the progress (both physical and financial) of local group initiatives and schemes.

- Provide corporate affairs support to local groups.

Time scales

Group to meet on an eight-weekly basis.

Composition

Production Strategy Manager (chair)

Area TSDMs

Public Affairs

BTP

Trespass and vandalism – local group

Purpose

Over a defined period local groups will report to the trespass and vandalism steering group to review identified problems or trends at specific locations, so as to target the zone's response to trespass and vandalism incidents in the most cost-effective and efficient manner.

Terms of reference

- Analyse trends in trespass and vandalism incidents by type.

- With the zone's customers and suppliers, develop and implement initiatives to lessen and eliminate trespass and vandalism throughout the area of responsibility.

- Develop plans maximising the effect of the resources available, putting forward cases to the steering group when additional resources or funding are necessary.

- Monitor the progress of initiatives and report to the steering group.

- Review the security of materials, including equipment and troughs at the line side, which trespassers could use to cause disruption and/or injury.

Time scale

To meet as required or as remitted by the steering group.

Composition

As remitted by the steering group but to comprise representatives of appropriate local Railtrack staff, its infrastructure maintenance contractor and principal customer. Chaired by the area TSDM.

Case Study 3 – Railtrack Scotland Loss Control Group remit

Frequency: Every quarter.

Duration: 3½ hours (variable according to Agenda).

Chair: Railtrack Scotland Production Manager. Safety and Standards Manager to deputise.

Attendance: Safety and/or operational professional heads from all interfacing Railway Group organisations, and BTP. The level of empowerment should be high enough for attendees to make strategic loss control decisions for their parent organisations where appropriate.

Format: There will be a series of approximately 15 to 20 minute presentations on previously agreed subjects with transferable value for other participating organisations.

Scope and purpose: The Loss Control Group aims to share best practice and 'lessons learned' about loss control, to launch crime prevention initiatives, to formulate and share Safety Plan issues and to provide each other with mutual aid and support.

Success criteria: Success will be measured by looking at the continued development of integrated safety management systems, measuring improvements in safety performance, encouraging common ownership and combined approaches to problem solving and fostering a 'can do' safety culture. Customer satisfaction can be measured by carrying out a 'hot debrief' of attendees at the end of each meeting and by circulating and assessing an annual customer satisfaction questionnaire.

Case study 4 – Midland Main Line

Objective: To assist Railtrack in reducing the instances of trespass and vandalism.

Dates: April 1996 – present.

Background: All train staff were briefed on the procedures to follow when they come across instances of trespass and vandalism.

Outcome: It is now possible to identify known trouble spots, thanks to better staff reporting of trespass and vandalism. Both Railtrack and BTP can target resources more effectively and thus reduce wastage.

3 – USE OF TECHNOLOGY AND PREVENTATIVE HARDWARE SYSTEMS

This section looks at some of the 'hardware' methods of preventing trespass and vandalism, such as fencing and CCTV.

37 The need for physical and other constraints on people trespassing on the railways is a peculiarly British one. The requirement that railways should be fenced was imposed at the time of the original construction due to pressure from landowners and farmers. Most other countries do not require fencing.

38 Over time, and particularly in recent years, legal and social attitudes have increasingly placed a preventative responsibility on the industry for controlling entry to the rail network. Measures to restrict or hinder entry to the network are very important.

Fencing

39 On an open line side, fencing is the obvious requirement. On most of the network, five-strand wire fencing is sufficient to meet the risk from humans and animals. In rural areas, however, trespass by animals can be sufficiently serious to justify enhanced fencing. Often the cost is borne by, or shared with, the adjacent landowner. The Polmont disaster in 1984, when 12 passengers were killed when a train was derailed after running into a herd of cattle, is a reminder that animal trespass can have catastrophic consequences. Damage and delay caused by trains striking large animals is a recurring feature in many parts of the country.

40 Most trespass occurs in urban areas, particularly around housing. Although most of the motives for trespass are non-malicious, trespassing imposes risks to the trespasser and cost and delay to railway operators. Damage to fencing for trespass purposes is vandalism and creates an opportunity for others to follow. All opportunities for unauthorised access can lead to trespass for malicious purposes.

41 Preventative measures need to be in keeping with the nature of the trespass. Some 'recreational' trespass can be deterred by modest enhancements to fencing, or with notices and household leaflets. 'Short cut' trespass prevention is more difficult: it needs to be sufficiently regular to justify providing an authorised railway crossing. In extreme cases, it may be appropriate to encourage the local authority to provide a footbridge. This is particularly the case where a housing development is on the opposite side of the railway from shopping or recreational centres.

42 Damage to trains and line-side equipment often comes from bridges or tunnel portals over the railway or from the sides of bridges. Installing higher, unclimbable parapets, fencing or enclosures over parapets and sidewalls can be effective. The attached design specifications from Railtrack (Case study 5) gives examples, while Case study 6 offers an approach to securing caging for bridges.

43 In some places even high-grade security fencing has been attacked. In these circumstances, it may be necessary to reinforce fencing with alarm systems or

CCTV. This is particularly the case in train depots and workshops, where trespass can be a precursor to vandalism or theft.

CCTV

44 The use of CCTV has spread rapidly in recent years and it is an increasingly appropriate method of controlling trespass and vandalism at stations, station car parks, depot/workshops and even on the open line side. Its use on trains, both internally for behaviour control and externally for viewing line-side trespass, is growing. Co-ordination with town centre CCTV systems can improve effectiveness and encourage closer community involvement. Conversely, introducing a town centre CCTV system can displace problems to the railway where CCTV coverage might not exist.

45 Technology now provides passive systems, which do not activate until a movement is detected. In this instance, lights and CCTV are activated and/or a monitoring operator is alerted to give a voice response over the public address system. Alternatively, you may find night vision cameras useful in circumstances where lighting is not appropriate or possible.

46 Good lighting that illuminates hidden and particularly dark areas is a very effective deterrent, particularly in car parks and stations. Where persistent problems occur, CCTV may act as a further deterrent or provide evidence for subsequent detection and prosecution.

47 The provision of real-time monitoring is a growing concern. Passive recording can be useful as evidence for prosecution but does not actively prevent the incident occurring. Continuous monitoring is expensive and does not necessarily provide observation and reaction to a specific incident, particularly if it is sudden or of short duration. Cardiff Railway Company's experiences with unmonitored and monitored systems at Caerphilly and Treforrest illustrate this (Case study 8). Case study 7 illustrates the benefits of continuous monitoring and help points with CCTV. The use of dummy CCTV cameras to control open line problem areas is illustrated in Case study 10.

48 Before installing a CCTV system, you should consider its purpose, the quality and reliability of the system and maintenance arrangements. BTP and other police forces are happy to provide guidelines on installing and operating CCTV.

49 ScotRail and Strathclyde Passenger Transport Executive (PTE) have developed a cost-effective system of interactive CCTV which uses internal railway telephone lines to transmit pictures to a monitoring centre. The system also enables the monitor operator to speak to a location through the station PA system and provides help points linked to the centre. In addition it has a direct link to the BTP Control Centre which can 'take over' the camera operation if an incident is identified.

50 Controlling entry to stations has become more difficult over recent years with station staff on duty less and less often. There is also a commercial desire to improve the ease of access to trains by removing barriers. However, this increases the risk of unauthorised and malicious access to the station and the line side.

51 Northern Spirit has developed a flexible station staffing structure which justifies posting staff, often with CCTV, at comparatively small stations.

52 London Underground continues to run a 'closed' system at most of its stations, and its new 'Prestige' ticketing system will extend that closed system. A number of franchised operators are installing barrier systems or manned access to reduce ticketless travel and to control unauthorised access (Case study 9).

53 An HSE Contract Research Report (No. 154/1997), *Risk to the Public at Unsupervised Stations*, looked at the particular dangers of children gaining access to unmanned stations. You need to display notices warning of the dangers of playing on stations and provide measures to control trespass from the platform to the railway line.

54 Control of vandalism and theft in car parks is particularly important for train operators as car users can be deterred from using rail services if they feel their cars are insecure or if they feel a threat to their own security in and around the car park. The accreditation system for car parks sets out criteria for design, lighting and surveillance. This system was initiated by the Association of Chief Police Officers and is administered by the Automobile Association. Case study 11 shows the benefits of accreditation. The Association of Train Operating Companies (ATOC) produced a Code of Practice which includes a commitment by all train operators to pursue car park accreditation.

55 A number of initiatives have been developed to protect trains from vandalism damage. Northern Spirit developed a protective film for single-glazed windows to reduce the risk of shattering from stone throwing. This may also be appropriate for double-glazed windows.

56 CCTV on trains is now being developed by a number of train operators, but no firm evidence that it works is yet available.

57 Emergency equipment on trains is sometimes misused. Connex South Eastern decided, after a risk assessment, that it would be safer to remove safety equipment from publicly accessible areas and instead keep it in places only readily available to staff.

58 One infrastructure contractor uses video filming on the front of a traction unit to monitor the condition of the track and the presence of line-side material.

Case study 5 – Railtrack

Design specification

Fencing philosophy

Security fencing deters some but not all of those tempted to trespass on and vandalise the railway. The determination of potential trespassers and vandals to overcome physical barriers varies according to a number of factors such as the availability of alternative routes around the railway and the local socio-economic culture. The principle also states that the harder it is get on to the railway, the more people will be deterred.

Fencing specification and general issues

Galvanised steel fence is the norm, though in some places it may be unsuitable for aesthetic reasons. Public objections can often be dealt with simply by painting the fence, though in more difficult cases other types of fence may have to be installed. Galvanised steel palisade fence should have a minimum specification that complies with British Standard BS 1722 (Part 12). It is highly recommended to fit the 'W' section rather than the 'D' section in the British Standard as it is stronger.

The issue of whether planning permission is required for fences over 2 m high is somewhat confused.

The August 1997 Line Standard, brought out as a result of recent Construction, Design and Management (CDM) regulations, requires that a full services search is done before foundations for fencing are dug. This can take some weeks and should be allowed for in planning time scales.

Types of fence

1.8 m palisade: This should be considered as the standard installation for security fencing. It is the cheapest, at £55 to £60 per fitted metre (1997/98 prices).

2.4 m palisade: This should be applied in the relatively limited areas where it is judged likely that access will be routinely gained over a 1.8 m fence or where there is evidence that this is happening once the shorter fence is installed. It has to be a matter of judgement whether the increased cost of a 2.4 m fence is outweighed by the performance risk. The current cost of installation is £65 to £70 per fitted metre.

3.1 m palisade: This tends only to be used for high security purposes such as around power signal boxes. The cost (at 1997/98 prices) is £75 to £90 per fitted metre.

Weld mesh: Weld mesh can be used in places where palisade is inappropriate, though the site has to be low risk in terms of likely damage. The advantages of weld mesh are that it is a relatively cheap step up from post and wire fence and it is more aesthetically pleasing than palisade. It can also be used on bridge parapets to prevent stones being dropped over the side. The disadvantage is that it is very attractive to thieves for domestic use. Prices start at £25 to £30 per fitted metre for the 1.8 m high and 2 mm thick specification.

Don't forget the gates

As mentioned above, the access requirements of production and infrastructure maintenance contractor (IMC) staff need to be taken into account. The current (1997/98) prices of gates are shown in the table below.

Type of gate (double)	1.8 m	2.4 m
Single	£600–£700	£700–£750
Double (for vehicular access)	£750–£950	£850–£1050

The cost of any fencing includes 'fans' so that it can properly butt-up to bridges and other feaures. The bewildering number of types makes it difficult to quote a price.

Anti-tamper measures

Where security fencing is attacked (with usually one or more struts fully or partially removed to gain access), an additional deterrence measure should be applied.

Axle grease or non-drying paint can be applied to the repaired area. It is important that this is applied so that members of the public cannot be accidentally contaminated. Warning signs should also be placed in a prominent position.

A third rail can be added to the bottom of the fence for added strength. A further, more expensive measure is to install a concrete plinth along the bottom. Fixings can also be enhanced. High tensile steel shear bolts can replace the standard fitting. As a final measure the fixings can be welded in place, though it is important to follow this up with another application of galvanised coating.

One of the benefits of security fencing is that it is easy to see where access is being gained. This helps BTP in surveillance and arrest operations.

17

Case study 6 – Railtrack South Zone

Bridge caging project: Railtrack South Zone has targeted what we believe to be the worst footbridges to be caged to reduce trespass and vandalism.

The zone appointed a project development manager. Eight of the bridges are owned by the local authority and are therefore managed by the outside parties section. Railtrack owns the other 14.

The problem: There are very few minutes' delay attributed to stone throwing and trespass and vandalism at individual footbridges. Often, the train crew do not notice stone throwing, or the incident is reported via the cab secure radio without delaying the train. Broken windows as a result of stone throwing are usually only discovered once the train reaches its terminal station or depot.

As the train is not actually delayed, it is difficult to justify funding on performance criteria. There is also no budget provision within the zone for this type of project: budget bids are rejected in favour of funding coming from Asset Maintenance Plan (AMP).

The solution: A paper on safety is being prepared for the Zone Investment Panel (ZIP). The paper will focus on the risk of injury or death to a train driver or passenger as a result of stone throwing or other acts of trespass or vandalism. It will also ask ZIP to consider the effect of a route blacking by drivers due to trains being bombarded, which may well happen if the number of incidents is not reduced.

Case study 7 – London Underground Ltd

Objective: To enhance customer and staff security within the Ladbroke Grove group of stations, which covers the area from Hammersmith to Paddington.

Date: 1998 – present.

Background: A central security room was provided at Ladbroke Grove station enabling all eight stations within the group to be monitored by CCTV and video recordings.

Secure areas and help points on each station allow communications between station platforms and the security room. The security room is permanently staffed, and staff are trained to respond to incidents accordingly.

Outcome: Incidents of crime within the group fell initially by 37% and the situation remains under control. However, some crime moved into the areas immediately outside the stations. Victims exiting the stations were followed once they were beyond the view of the staff and cameras. The CCTV network is being extended to cover the area outside the station where necessary or feasible.

Case study 8 – Cardiff Railway Company CCTV trial at Treforrest railway station

Background

Cardiff Railway Company (CRC) is obliged under the franchise plan to install CCTV at a minimum of five stations by October 1998 and across the rest of the network over the remaining franchise term. Many CCTV systems are available, each with advantages and disadvantages.

CRC studied a number of installations looking at the monitoring commitment in terms of resources, ease of manual control and response level to external stimuli.

System chosen

After a careful assessment of what was needed, CRC selected the Remote Watch PRO system made by Cyclops System Plc (UK) (now ASL Systems).

The system is flexible and can be upgraded at low cost because it is based on standard PCs. No special equipment is required. It is modestly priced compared to other systems.

The hard disk recording medium has considerable duration and quality advantages over videotape and does not require daily changing. This is a major factor for CRC, which has many unstaffed locations. As the hardware is PC-based, many different presets, devices and alarms can be programmed into a multi-media system.

Automatic networking and/or individual site touring is easily managed, via pre-programmed drop-down menus. Manual control on demand is a built-in feature.

CRC carried out a physical trial to test the limits of the technology and make sure it met their needs.

Location

A location known to suffer high levels of damage and graffiti would seem a prime candidate for an installation. However, the trial was primarily intended to test the technology without going into extended monitoring of the test site.

Treforrest is within the Pontypridd district and has a small adjacent community. The station principally serves the Pontypridd campus of the University of Wales.

During term time the campus is open from 8.30 am to 9.00 pm. A high proportion of the students is female. The university remains open through the summer holidays and runs many special courses for fee-paying students, particularly those from the Latin countries of the European Union. These factors gave CRC an opportunity to measure customer perception across a wide spectrum of social, ethnic and cultural groups.

Many customers had complained about loiterers using obscene language, making sexual remarks or invitations to lone females and drinking and fighting. The staff reported finding condoms, bottles and cans and evidence of drug use on a regular basis. There were reports of the park and ride car park and adjacent roadway being used as a racing circuit by 'bikers' and 'boy racers'.

Costs

The total installation cost was £10 000. Careful planning could have reduced the cost. The speed of the installation at Treforrest meant using external sub-contractors to drill the pole bases and fill them with pre-mixed concrete, which added to the cost. In addition, a particularly sophisticated and expensive pan, tilt and zoom (PTZ) camera was installed, mainly to save time. It performs functions that otherwise could only be done by several fixed (and cheaper) cameras.

The cost of the HQ installation was £3 500. However, the base receiver was pre-programmed to manage a network of up to 30 sites and therefore is not a repeatable cost.

Glitches

CRC experienced only two small technical problems. After four days the site modem refused to co-operate with its HQ brother and a replacement was provided and the polycarbonate bowl on the PTZ camera was not waterproof. A replacement gasket sealed the unit effectively.

Publicity

The project generated an enormous amount of regional media interest. BBC Wales and the commercial channels broadcast news items and the media were shown the local installation, although they were denied access to the HQ monitoring location. Each news slot held interviews with customers who were overwhelmingly in favour of the project.

This customer perception has been strongly reinforced by subsequent surveys. Security is a commercial issue that transport providers ignore at their cost.

Test results

The test proved successful. Staff reported that no materials, other than cigarette ends and some ordinary refuse, had been found since the test began. During out of hours visits there was a total absence of loiterers, boy racers and bikers and there were no complaints from university students of either gender. No vehicle damage was reported, and there was no graffiti or damage to the station. Station issues per period before CCTV were 3753; since CCTV was introduced, they have risen to 5807.

One car was reported stolen from the car park during October 1997. It was not possible to identify the perpetrator, and CRC concluded that the crime had been carried out by a professional thief.

One complaint was received about someone skateboarding in the Treforrest park and ride area at 3.00 am on 21 November 1997. The individual had left by the time BTP arrived.

Additional features

Further cost savings are possible at each installed site. The Remote-watch PRO system can manage and control a wide range of devices, intruder alarms and security locks. Monitoring costs can be reduced if a company has its own CCTV control, as no outside agency monitoring is then needed.

The public address system can be run on a side band of the CCTV system if desired.

Conclusion

The technology proved reliable and effective through a range of weather conditions. The system is easily managed with the tools provided. Replay quality is almost broadcast standard although the live monitored picture at CRC HQ is slightly slow, due to lack of bandwidth. This will be remedied when the common infrastructure comes on line. Directors of CRC and Prism Railways Board among others have seen demonstrations of the system.

CCTV Caerphilly survey results

CCTV statistics

A study of four systems – Cardiff City, Pontypridd Town, the Gateshead Metro Centre and Manchester Metro system – showed that a properly designed and well publicised system can bring about a reduction of up to 90% of reportable crime in the short term. In the long term, reductions of up to 80% can be maintained.

Together with Mid-Glamorgan County Council, CRC arranged for a system to be installed in the park and ride area at Caerphilly.

Survey report on CCTV at Caerphilly park and ride

No control centre is provided, nor are the cameras controlled manually. It is a 'stand alone', partially monitored system with movement detectors activated by a time clock.

Object of survey

To assess any increase in the usage of the park and ride facility and in ticket sales at Caerphilly, together with any impact on crime, after providing CCTV.

Site visits carried out on the following dates prior to the installation:
Monday 3 April (7.30 am)............................**Usage 15%**
Wednesday 5 April (4.00 pm).....................**Usage 20%**
Monday 10 April (7.30 am)........................**Usage 20%**
Wednesday 12 April (4.00 pm) ....**Usage 17.5%**

The system went live on Friday 21 April 1995.

Site visits carried out after installation and prior to any publicity:
Wednesday 10 May (7.30 am) ....**Usage 20%**
Monday 15 May (4.00 pm).........................**Usage 25%**
Monday 5 June (4.00 pm).......................**Usage 53.5%**
Friday 16 June (1.30 pm) ....**Usage 66%**

Ticket sales before and after installation:
Average of 10 weeks from 29 May 1995 to 2 June 1995

	Before	After
Monday	182	230 + 48 = 26%
Tuesday	168	199 + 31 = 18.4%
Wednesday	181	198 + 17 = 10%
Thursday	165	200 + 45 = 27%
Friday	183	194 + 11 = 6%

Car-related crimes reported
1 January 1995 – 31 April 1995   **20 incidents**
Car-related crimes reported
1 May 1995 – August 18 1995   **3 incidents**

Site visits carried out on:
Wednesday 9 August (4.00 pm)................**Usage 75%**
Friday 11 August (4.00 pm)......................**Usage 80%**
Monday 14 August (4.00 pm)...................**Usage 85%**
Wednesday 16 August (4.00pm)...............**Usage 90%**

Conclusions

- The system proved invaluable in reducing car-related crime, which is estimated to cost an average £800 per incident (figures provided by the Insurance Association).

- Installing the system has so far saved £14 000 and ongoing savings of £1000 each week there is no incident.

- The effect on potential rail customers is not quantifiable. There was a dramatic increase in patronage of the car park. However, the car park is adjacent to a popular shopping centre. We do not yet know if this will lead to more people using the railway.

- The system provided CRC with valuable data, attracted positive media coverage and reinforced the point that we care about our customers and their property.

21

Case study 9 – Connex South Central

Objectives

- To reduce the level of crime and eradicate incidents of vandalism to trains and stations on the South London Metro Area.

- To make customers using our services and stations feel safer, thereby increasing passenger numbers and revenue.

Dates

From February 1997 to the present.

Background

Analysis from BTP crime figures showed that West Croydon station was noted for its high level of crime. To tackle both this and ticketless travel, ticket barrier checks were reintroduced in May 1997. Within weeks, the level of reported crime incidents fell by about 90% and revenue increased by about 11%.

There was a high level of incidents of vandalism and graffiti on the Mitcham Junction to Sutton line affecting all intermediary stations. Nearly all customers, rail user groups, local MPs and borough councils surveyed about this line thought the situation was getting worse. To combat this, partnerships were forged with the community safety sections of the local councils, Youth Awareness programmes, the youths responsible for the vandalism and graffiti, and Railtrack's Trespass and Vandalism Group.

Outcome

All vandalised stations were fitted with CCTV. Other measures included installing better fencing and lighting and holding a graffiti festival at Wallington station on 19 October 1997. This involved established graffiti artists from the area, across the country and even from the continent. The festival was featured on all the national TV networks. BTP was not involved and at the time of writing vandalism and graffiti on this line has been eradicated.

Passenger numbers have increased by about 10% and revenue increased by around 15%.

By September 1997, all parties involved in the initial survey thought the problem had been eradicated.

Case study 10 – Railtrack

Objective

To investigate whether dummy CCTV cameras have a deterrent effect, using three different locations – Abercynon station, Bedminster and Ebbw Junction – to determine effectiveness.

Duration of trial

Three months.

Result

Abercynon station is an unstaffed valley line station that had been subject to persistent trespass and vandalism activity, which included youths gaining access to the railways via the platform ramp. The camera was placed on a pole overlooking the platform and focused on the waiting shelter. During the test period, reported incidents decreased from an average of 13 to 2 (a reduction of 84%), and the equipment was undamaged.

At Bedminster there had been persistent incursions by people damaging fencing and trespassing on the railway. The camera was placed on a steel pole and targeted at the points of incursion. There was a 55% reduction in reported incidents and the camera was not damaged.

Ebbw Junction is a large junction site that once had many more lines than it does now. As a result, there is a large expanse of derelict ground, which is one of the most incident-prone locations within the zone. There was no decrease in incidents at this station. The camera was damaged after 12 days and removed altogether after 19 days.

Considerations

The cameras in small locations that were targeted on precise areas had a deterrent effect. The one at Ebbw Junction that was monitoring an open site did not.

Conclusion

Dummy CCTV is only effective where it can be protected and targeted at a specific problem and site.

Case study 11 – Thameslink

Objective: To upgrade Bedford car park to AA standard in order to reduce crime and maximise revenue opportunities.

APCOA (car park managers), Bedford Borough Council, Bedford Commuters Association, Bedfordshire Police and Railtrack provided additional input.

Background: Car parks and their management are an integral part of the business, providing an additional facility to our customers. Surveys showed that the main issue for users was vehicle security. Bedford Commuters' Association took an active lead in encouraging security improvements and a strategy was developed to upgrade Bedford car park to AA standard. This included:

- upgrading the CCTV;
- improving CCTV surveillance;
- installing improved lighting;
- refencing the perimeter of the car park;
- continued car park management by APCOA.

The benefits of the scheme were:

- AA Standard Accreditation;
- improved vehicle security;
- a safer car park for users;
- reduction of vandalism to premises;
- installation of CCTV which provides footage which can be used as evidence in court;
- working with the community;
- increased patronage, currently at 82%;
- rationalisation of revenue from improved service.

The first phase of the scheme started in January 1998.

Figure 3 – Train fires 1976–1997/98

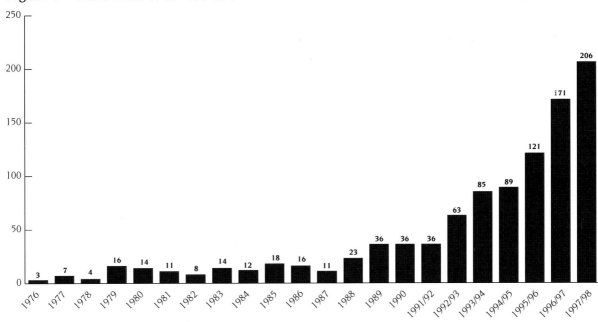

Increase in fires shown after 1987 reflects the inclusion of small incidents such as smouldering cigarette ends which had not been counted prior to Kings X

the network and increased cost, since the effects of the incident on employees and the infrastructure have to be managed.

6 Railtrack has primary responsibility for managing the security of the main rail network infrastructure. The company recognised this in its management focus on trespass and vandalism and has commissioned a major study on the problem to identify priority areas which will provide support for identifying and focusing on priorities. However, trespass and vandalism are issues for the entire industry and all members need to work together to contain the problem. There are some elements for individuals to address and others where a multi-party approach is needed.

Causes of trespass

7 Trespass means entering someone else's property unlawfully. Although it does not always lead to acts of vandalism, trespass on railway property can be a significant health and safety risk. There are different reasons why trespass takes place and safety rules are violated.

8 Routine trespass may occur when the safety rules are seen as too restrictive or as not applying to the perpetrator. The trespass may save time or energy and there may be a perceived lack of enforcement of rules. Examples include walking through the 'no exit' passage in a station, taking a short cut across the railway, or using railway property for recreational purposes. Such routine violations can involve knowingly taking risks in the belief that the benefits outweigh the risks.

9 Situational trespass occurs when breaking the rule is considered necessary. Typical reasons are time pressure (someone is late for the train); weather conditions; the time of day (preferring not to walk down a dark subway); or physical constraints (trying to get a heavy pram down steps).

10 Exceptional reasons for trespasses occur rarely and only when something goes wrong. Typical examples are a parent trespassing to rescue a child, or a dog owner retrieving their dog from the track.

11 Trespassing 'for kicks' is more common in younger people who may congregate in large groups on or near railway property. The perpetrators are aware that they are breaking the rules and may indeed seek the excitement that this involves. They may wish to see how far they can go before being caught, to see what will happen or to gain the approval of their peers.

12 The initiatives outlined in later chapters will help to detect and prevent many of these trespasses. Some types of trespassing, especially 'for kicks', are the most difficult to control. In such instances, a multi-faceted approach which looks at combining prevention measures such as detection, deterrence, education and environmental design, is particularly important. This multi-faceted approach is well demonstrated in the Feltham area, where the rail industry works with the community (Case study 1).

Defining vandalism

13 Vandalism may be defined as the intentional destruction, damage or disfigurement of public or private property, leading to a reduction in the functionality and economic or aesthetic value of an object or area. People typically associate the term 'vandalism' with ideas like 'malicious damage', 'rowdyism', 'blind wish to wreck', 'destructive violence', 'senseless rowdyism', and 'criminal youth'. These associations assume that we know something about those who carry out acts of vandalism and why they do so. Yet there are different types of vandalism.

14 Acquisitive vandalism involves property damage and includes offences such as breaking into cars and telephone coin boxes.

15 Tactical vandalism is designed to draw attention to the perpetrator or their wishes, for example farmers dumping a pile of manure at the town hall.

16 Vindictive vandalism aims for revenge on a person or institution. An example might be someone breaking a car aerial in the course of a personal argument.

17 Play vandalism occurs typically during a game and is not intentional. An example is broken playground equipment that has been used other than for its intended purpose.

18 Malicious vandalism involves acts that are intentional and directed against public or private property but which usually result in no material gain for the perpetrator. Examples include arson in telephone kiosks and slitting seat cushions on public transport. Factors here can include peer pressure.

The purpose of this book

19 This publication looks mainly at preventing and reducing acts of malicious vandalism on public transport systems. The reasons for such vandalism are puzzling, but researchers have identified *who* performs such deeds, *where* and some of the possible reasons *why*. While this research is limited, we have included references to any relevant findings or ideas in the 'Further information' section at the end of the publication.

20 The problems posed by trespass and vandalism have long been recognised by the industry and over the years there have been many initiatives to combat the problems. The fact that the problems have not been reduced does not imply a lack of concern or effort by the industry. However, there is evidence to suggest that initiatives are not always co-ordinated and that experiences are not always readily shared. The overall effectiveness of initiatives has not been quantified.

21 The purpose of this book is to assist companies operating in the rail industry by providing examples of practices which have already been adopted. We demonstrate the effectiveness of these practices and highlight the lessons learned so far. It is not intended to be prescriptive, since solutions will vary according to specific circumstances. It is intended to provide practical help in focusing efforts on the measures likely to be most effective when dealing with trespass and vandalism.

4 – PREVENTATIVE OPERATIONAL SYSTEMS

This section suggests some of the operational arrangements an organisation can develop and put in place in order to deal with trespass and vandalism.

59 Appropriate operational arrangements make it easier to control trespass and vandalism. At the simplest level, immediate and consistent reporting of incidents by railway employees helps to deter trespass and vandalism. It also provides valuable information about the nature and extent of problems.

Security guards

60 Signallers at Railtrack Midland Zone have been patrolling sensitive line side areas. Railtrack has adopted this initiative nationally under the name Operation Scarecrow (Case study 15). Involving staff with train operators and infrastructure contractors could reinforce this initiative.

61 The role of maintenance contractors' staff in observing trespass and vandalism and noting where line side material might be used for malicious acts of vandalism cannot be stressed too highly. Maintaining security of access points is particularly important.

62 Line-side equipment and buildings are prone to damage and graffiti attacks. GTRM (an infrastructure company) has developed a reflective speed warning board fixed between the tracks which minimises the risk of removal, damage or defacement of line-side signs.

63 Infrastructure controllers and their maintenance and renewal contractors can minimise vandalism opportunities by ensuring that all materials are properly safeguarded. Scrap and surplus materials should be removed promptly.

Security operation

64 There are a number of case studies demonstrating the benefits of deploying security staff on stations and on trains. Case study 14 illustrates the benefits of a company security operation. Careful training and briefing will ensure a consistent and professional approach to the railway environment and problems of vandalism on stations and trains will be considerably reduced. Case studies 12 and 13 show that targeted deployment can be particularly effective in known locations, on specific trains, or at times of the day, week or season when disruptive and malicious behaviour occurs. Training for guards, ticket collectors and station staff can improve their effectiveness in preventing vandalism on trains and stations.

Help points

65 Help points are primarily intended to improve passengers' sense of personal security, but the system can also be used for reporting instances of misbehaviour, vandalism or trespass. London Underground and ScotRail's experiences are described in section 3.

66 Similarly, train and station staff can use attack alarms and personal radios to summon assistance in the event of attacks or malicious behaviour. Nexus, the Tyne and Wear Metro operator, has developed a lateral approach to rowdy behaviour and vandalism by youths on its stations. It plays classical music, which appears to act as an effective deterrent to the youths.

Case study 12 – Connex South Eastern

Objectives

■ To reduce the level of vandalism to trains on the North Kent line between Dartford and Deptford.

■ To reduce the delays caused by vandalism on trains.

■ To make passengers feel safer in the evenings.

Dates

9 June 1997 to the present.

Background

A high level of vandalism was affecting rolling stock on the North Kent route (Classes 465 and 466). Analysis showed that many of the incidents happened after 3.00 pm. Nearly 50% of passengers said they thought vandalism and graffiti were getting worse. To combat this, security officers were employed on the trains from 3.00 pm until the last train, seven days a week.

The officers worked in pairs and were trained by a security company, BTP and ourselves. They had assignment instructions and diagrams of specific services covering almost every train. They carried mobile phones with pre-programmed numbers for the police, the service delivery centre and each other.

Outcome

■ Three times as many people felt safer travelling after the scheme had been operating for six months.

■ After six months there was a ten-fold reduction in the perception that vandalism and graffiti were getting worse.

■ There was a four-fold reduction in the perception that drunkenness and rowdy behaviour is getting worse.

■ There was a 40% reduction in incidents of vandalism on trains.

■ We saved up to £10 000 per week in damage to rolling stock and delays to services.

■ The availability of rolling stock improved. Security officers reported problems immediately, which meant they could be rectified quickly.

■ The officers worked well with Connex staff and with BTP and the scheme was extended to other routes from April 1998.

Case study 13 – Thameslink/British Transport Police

Objective

To win back the Wimbledon loop from vandals and enhance public perception of security on the Wimbledon loop.

Abbey Partnership Policing Initiative, BTP and Worcester Polytechnic Institute, Mass., USA all provided additional input.

Background

The Wimbledon loop stations have become very run down over the last decade, with town centre CCTV installations pushing the vandals on to the next soft target, the railway. The resulting vandalism and graffiti had an adverse effect on customers, who felt threatened, and prevented people using the service which in turn encouraged the vandals.

Combined with the fact that some of the stations are unmanned, the lack of passengers is also encouraging other criminals to move into the area. There is a trend towards more serious crime. Staff safety was also a problem, with assaults on station and on-train staff.

The Abbey Partnership sponsored students from Worcester Polytechnic Institute who researched and wrote *Safer Stations, An Interactive Qualifying Project Report*. This report showed that fear of crime was a key issue. Levels of reported crime, although difficult to attribute to locations, were not as high as they were generally perceived to be. However, the situation was likely to continue to deteriorate if not addressed as a matter of urgency. The survey made several recommendations, one of which led to the introduction of security guards.

The security guards received full training and started their patrols on 10 November 1997. Their work schedules were designed to give maximum coverage during the hours when most problems occur.

Benefits

- Diminished fear of crime
- Improved security at stations
- Improved security on trains
- Cleaner, graffiti-free stations
- Increased revenue collected by on-train service supervisors
- More customers travelling
- Fewer assaults
- New working relationships and contacts with community organisations leading to the development of related schemes
- Continued development of the Wimbledon loop
- Positive publicity and media coverage.

A follow-up survey from Worcester Polytechnic Institute, designed to assess the impact of the measures on public awareness and satisfaction, was scheduled for April 1998. As with the first project, Thameslink will provide support and assistance throughout. The final results of their findings were produced in June 1998. Crime Concern will carry out a further evaluation later in the year.

Case study 14 – Mercy Travel Limited (MTL) security and audit

Report for period 3 (2–28 June 1998)

The main areas of operation were in the Newcastle, Sunderland and Middlesbrough triangle. There were also visits to stations in the surrounding areas, including Yorkshire, Bradford and Halifax.

A high-profile uniform presence was operating at Chester Le Street and Sunderland stations. Covert operatives were also working in the same areas.

Thirteen reports were passed to the Northern Spirit prosecutions officer for further investigation. The reports submitted are for various public order offences including people found urinating on the stations.

In the next period, regional support unit (RSU) will concentrate on those areas highlighted by the Northern Spirit monthly crime analysis report.

RSU also took part in a one-day induction course with BTP at York. The course helped RSU build stronger links with BTP in the north-east.

Station visits	Ejected	Arrests	Instructed	Fare evasions	Train patrols
151	104	1	47	2	37

Report for period 4 (1–31 July 1998)

The main areas of operation were in the Yorkshire, Hough Green and Widnes areas. During the period, RSU was issued with trackside safety (PTS) certificates and two officers passed their 'PICOW' course. After several meetings with Leeds BTP, we were invited to join them on a 'Q-train'. BTP patrols these trains in order to catch, caution and prosecute trespassers.

Although RSU were only present as observers, the exercise was very informative. However, we did offer our services when BTP was understaffed. The team was invited to Sankey station, where there was a fatality. There were enough police officers present and the team moved on to Warrington station to offer help to the station staff who displayed a commendably professional attitude and approach.

We passed 25 reports on public order offences and trespass to the Northern Spirit prosecution officer.

In August, RSU was invited on a joint operation on Bradford Interchange.

Ejected	Trespass	Fare evasions	Public order	Instructions
91	37	2	2	91

Case study 15 – Operation Scarecrow

Background

In September 1996, a steering group was set up by the then Public Affairs Manager to tackle trespass and vandalism in the zone. The group included the Area Production Manager (APM) along with various representatives from contracts, performance, infrastructure management and BTP.

Up until December, the group was fairly active and had already decided on a strategy prioritising six areas in the zone. These are Stockingford, Stetchford, Adderley Park, Clay Cross, Peartree and Leicester South. Each had site visits to identify fencing defects, site improvements, local schools, access and egress. It was decided that more direct action was needed in the short term to tackle high-risk areas.

The group decided to look at a project initiated on Great Western Zone that sent rapid response staff to prioritised areas at specific times. The project had limited success and Railtrack Midlands decided to develop the idea.

Objectives

- To reduce the risk of unsafe acts. Although performance is important, safety has always been the main objective. Since data was collected in 1994, safety risks have increased due mainly to objects being placed on the line.

- To improve customer performance. This will improve customer confidence in the company. Although performance has steadily improved since April 1994, it is obvious that the Easter period can undo a great amount of hard work.

- To improve staff awareness. Although production staff throughout the zone are aware of trespass and vandalism incidents and have front-line experience in dealing with them, they need more commercial awareness as well as more awareness of the procedures for delay attribution and the effect on the customer. This project aims to develop such awareness.

- Instil customer confidence. If the above objectives are achieved, Railtrack will be able to show customers that measures are in place to reduce trespass and vandalism in the zone, which is costly for both staff and customers.

Signallers

Staff from the signalling grades are the first link in the chain when it comes to dealing with incidents. They have a reasonable knowledge of the area and they know line-side procedures. In addition, staff who had not been employed 'out on site' would gain valuable experience.

Birmingham APM area was selected for the initial stages of the project, as it contains three of the high-risk areas. Also, due to the dense rail network in the West Midlands, mobility and distance would be less of a problem. After the success of the 1997 initiative, the project was rolled out across the whole zone for the 1998/99 financial year.

In early February 1997, APM invited applications from all signallers in the area. Within two weeks more than 40 signallers – 25% of the workforce – had responded. All applicants were seen by either the Area Safety and Performance Manager (ASPM) or their local manager, and a final list was drawn up. The same happened in 1998 when the project went zone-wide, with over 150 signallers applying to take part in the programme.

Groups consisted of three people. One group was employed at any one time, the members being chosen from six available and trained signallers. This made the roster as flexible as possible.

The signallers ranged from grades 3–8, ensuring fairness and a broad range of experience. Signallers also came from different areas of the West Midlands, which guaranteed a wide range of local knowledge and expertise.

All the successful applicants had a positive attitude towards the industry and definite ideas on the subject, which proved invaluable as the project progressed.

Training

The signallers were sent on an extensive training programme, which was endorsed by the risk assessment in February 1997.

All staff needed full 'Person In Charge of Works' (PICOW) certification and had to attain certain first aid skills. They were also given full anti-aggression training to help them deal with the public. Commercial and performance-related briefings by the ASPM were supported by the Zone Production Manager.

However, the most important issue was to get staff out into the area. In early March, all six spent one week with the relevant signalling manager, concentrating on access points and procedures.

The project went live on 24 March 1997. Although this was the last week of period 13, the project coincided with one of the worst periods for trespass and vandalism: the Easter break and the school holidays.

The 1998 training programme incorporated the lessons learned in 1997. Twenty-two signallers attended a four-day training programme which emphasised risk assessment. Simplifying systems for reporting hazards has helped staff prioritise work and eradicate duplication.

Area prioritisation

We produced a strict timetable before the project went live to make sure that the 18 areas selected were visited at the right frequency and times for optimum impact. Signallers provided data from the previous 12 months, and we also used delay attribution and control logs. In 1998, the zone used a points system to select 60 known hot-spots. They then decided how often each would be visited. The points system worked like this:

Number of incidents x minutes lost (control logs, delay attribution)
Rated 1–5 in importance (5 = high)

+

Strategic importance of the area (number of train operating companies and frequency of service)
Rated 1–5 in importance (5 = high)

The two scores were added together and an area league table was drawn up, with the 18 areas divided into three groups of six. Group A was very high risk. Group C was important, but relatively low risk and low impact.

The group would be active for three days a week for eight weeks, providing 24 active days in 1997 and 56 in 1998. All signallers would work eight-hour shifts, with the first shift starting at 10.00 am and the last finishing at 9.00 pm. The earlier shift was designed for weekends and Bank Holidays and the late shift for weekdays. Working after 9.00 pm would threaten signallers' safety, and the service is greatly reduced at this time anyway.

Procedures

The signallers had four objectives:

- to contact the controlling signal box;
- to summon assistance (BTP emergency link instigated);
- to assess the situation and the area;
- to contact Zone Control.

The group would be equipped with a pager and mobile phone and a high quality camera and camcorder for obtaining evidence.

All production staff that would be involved in an incident, from control staff to BTP, were briefed through their liaison officer.

A standard daily location log was also produced, giving details of hazards in the area, locations visited and trains affected. From this a daily log was produced for all interested parties. The results were forwarded to the area contracts managers who could then use them as a blueprint for action with the contractor if required. Any photographic evidence obtained would also be supplied.

Media campaign

The Public Affairs Manager initiated a campaign coinciding with the first Bank Holiday. In 1997, he sent information to nearly every household in the region. In 1998, the same information was sent out across the country. In 1998, there were 7 television interviews, over 50 radio interviews and preparations made for a fly-on-the-wall documentary by the BBC. The success of the campaign was a key factor in the overall success of the project.

Measurement

The project's success depended on the accuracy of our measurement tools. We looked at previous figures from trespass and vandalism incidents in comparative periods and for the whole, control log data for measuring the types of activity involved and the number of potentially high-risk incidents. Looking at how much money had been saved following the adoption of these measures was a useful way of gauging their success. We also looked at the trends which emerged in 1997.

Results from 1995 and 1996

The Railtrack Midlands Performance Analyst collated data taken from the Birmingham APM area in 1995 and 1996. This was processed and fed into the 1998 programme.

The figures were similar for periods 1 and 2 in previous years, which take into account the Easter period. There was a general increase in minutes lost, reaching a peak during the school holidays. For nearly every period since April 1994, annual comparisons of the same periods indicate a steady increase in minutes lost in high-risk areas. The data we used takes into account weather conditions and the number of Bank Holidays.

Results from 1997

During periods 1 and 2 we achieved a decrease in minutes lost for the first time since 1994. Although not startling, these figures represent the whole APM area as well as areas not considered high risk.

Period 13 was one of the worst periods ever for the APM Birmingham area. In two major incidents, units were crippled because of objects on the line at

Adderley Park and Lea Hall. The group found this particularly frustrating as these incidents occurred during the first week of the campaign and group members had almost succeeded in preventing one of the incidents.

Results from 1998

In 1998, we were unable to reduce the number of minutes' delay in the Birmingham and Euston areas. However, other areas did improve. There are a number of reasons for this:

- Fatalities rose by 30% in 1998. Each fatality cost an average of 1100 minutes. In periods 1 and 2 there were three more fatalities than in the previous year.

- In period 1 there were two Bank Holidays compared to one in the previous year. On Bank Holidays there is an average of 7000 minutes' delay in the zone, as opposed to 2700 minutes on any normal weekday.

- Although the number of minutes' delay was slightly higher in 1998, with a 12% increase on 1997, after fatalities and Bank Holidays are taken into account the figure would in fact have been 11% lower.

- The number of reported incidents in the zone was down by 48% in 1998, achieving a risk reduction that was much greater than anticipated.

High-risk area comparison top 10

In period 1 in 1996, 827 minutes were lost to trespass and vandalism in the top 10 high-risk areas in the Birmingham area. However, in period 1 in 1997 there was a significant reduction, with only 270 minutes lost. In period 2 in 1996, 492 minutes were lost in the same areas, whereas in 1997 only 194 minutes were lost.

Analysis of the 1998 data for the whole zone will show that 77% of high-risk areas reduced both the numbers of minutes lost to trespass and vandalism and the number of incidents. Some areas not previously identified as high risk did make the top 20 half-way through the project, and Operation Scarecrow was then initiated there as well.

THE MURALS
ON THIS STATION
ARE A YOUTH
AND COMMUNITY
OUTREACH
INITIATIVE
THEY WERE
COMMISSIONED
BY THAMESLINK

INVESTING
IN YOUR

LOCAL
STATION.

5 – ENVIRONMENTAL DESIGN

Finding ways to improve the physical environment will help prevent – or at least significantly reduce – trespass and vandalism.

The environment and acts of vandalism

67 Some objects and places are particularly vulnerable to acts of malicious vandalism. These include:

- playgrounds and parks;

- school buildings and leisure centres;

- public transport;

- public buildings such as churches and museums;

- inner city areas and their fitments, such as street lamps and telephone boxes;

- residential buildings.

68 These places have certain common characteristics which can make them particularly vulnerable to damage and destruction.

69 They are public or community buildings rather than personal or private property. Large anonymous accessible areas are 'semi-public' or 'no-man's land' for which no identifiable person appears to be responsible. The area may be seen as being owned by an anonymous organisation. This lack of perceived 'care' for an environment is one of the most important factors. Damage to residential buildings usually occurs in areas which are out of sight of the residents, especially areas which appear neglected or in a poor state of repair. Often, the more neglected an area appears the more likely it is to be vandalised.

70 The environment measures have been drawn up with these considerations in mind. Making areas and buildings less anonymous by encouraging groups or individuals to assume responsibility for their care is a successful strategy, particularly in the case of school buildings. Maintaining and repairing damaged objects and removing graffiti may help to discourage further vandalism in areas which have already been affected. Objects may be designed so they are easy to remove and replace ('soft targets') as well as being hard to damage ('hard targets'). Finally, when choosing objects and buildings for public or semi-public areas it is helpful to consider whether they could be damaged 'in an interesting way'. If so, it is highly likely that such damage will occur.

Station design

71 Many former British Rail and London Underground stations have inherited design features from Victorian builders. These features can make access difficult for passengers and staff and make it hard to control vandalism. Many are too fundamental to be altered and in most cases rebuilding is impractical. Many stations, however, can be improved by modest redesign, particularly when major refurbishment or development is taking place. Better design, lighting and landscaping can improve station approaches and car parks (see Case study 17). Case study 16 shows that disorderly behaviour and vandalism occur in rural as well as urban areas and that redesign can improve the situation.

72 The design of new stations needs to take into account not just their accessibility but also their vulnerability to vandalism and graffiti attacks. New equipment is often a particular target for vandals and graffiti 'artists'. Clear design guidelines are needed.

Graffiti

73 Graffiti attacks are a particular problem for railway operators. It can be dangerous for the perpetrators, and graffiti increases the sense of a lack of control and security for passengers and staff.

74 Removing graffiti quickly helps discourage further attacks. A number of train operators choose not to put trains with graffiti into service.

75 Case study 19 shows that graffiti can be removed rapidly and effectively from station buildings and structures.

76 Preventing graffiti is obviously more effective than removing it. Controlling access is one means of prevention. However, BTP has found that controlling access can simply present a challenge to the perpetrators. Access control, therefore, needs to be comprehensive.

77 Murals and other decorative surfaces can reduce the incidence of graffiti, particularly if they are done in conjunction with the local community. Case study 18 and Case study 19 both illustrate this point.

78 Graffiti on line-side structures is harder to combat. It is arguably the most important area to tackle, given the trespass risks to the perpetrators and the adverse effect it has on railway users. Vegetation 'drapery' on vertical walls can cover the surface, and planting thorny or prickly shrubbery can act as a deterrent. Graffiti attacks on operational structures such as relay rooms and modules can really only be addressed by preventing access or by removing the structure.

Line side

79 The line-side environment can encourage trespass and vandalism. Much of the urban railway runs through areas of industrial dereliction and difficult housing. In many cases railway operators have reduced the land requirement for the operational railway, leaving large areas of unused and derelict lands, often with buildings, structures and materials which add to the dereliction. The uncontrolled growth of trees, bushes and shrubs can provide cover for trespassers and vandals. Clearing vegetation and materials from surplus land could be a cost-effective way of reducing problems in some areas. Conversely, planting 'aggressive' species of thorn bushes can inhibit access. The Essex Police leaflet contains some useful advice.

80 In 1986 British Rail initiated a major scheme to remove and secure line-side material. Operation Cleansweep was triggered by incidents like the derailment at West Ealing in London. The operation removed material likely to be vandalised and improved the environment. Avoiding the accumulation of line-side material is an important element of infrastructure maintenance and renewal contracts. It may be worth making a 'clean sweep' from time to time. Case study 20 outlines the current Railtrack Project Vista.

81 Removing redundant and derelict line-side and station buildings, huts and structures is a crucial part of clearing line-side material. They are places where trespassers can congregate and removing them reduces the problem and improves the appearance of the environment.

82 Several areas around the country have launched initiatives to improve the line-side environment, with some significant improvements.

83 Litter by the side of the line adds to the sense of dereliction and encourages further anti-social attacks on the railway. Fly-tipping is a major problem in some locations and Case study 21 shows how

improved fencing can help. Existing legislation and contractual commitments for litter control should be consistently complied with to reduce vandalism. Particular problems can occur in landfill sites and it may be helpful to seek the assistance of the local authority or Environment Agency office.

Case study 16 – Central Trains/Railtrack/British Transport Police

Objective: To prevent youths visiting Tywyn station and causing nuisance and danger to the local community.

Dates: 1996/97.

Background: A large number of youths used to gather at this unmanned rural station, annoying local residents and trespassing by using the lines as a short cut between the town centre and a housing estate. They also used the station car park as a 'race track', causing nuisance and danger.

The local police, residents and authority worked with Central Trains and Railtrack and erected palisade fencing to minimise trespass. Speed ramps and bollards were also placed in the station car park. These efforts were supplemented with high profile policing.

Outcome: The measures eradicated the problem.

Case study 17 – Lambeth Public Transport Group

Objective

To initiate safety and security measures at Wandsworth Road and Clapham High Street stations to improve the 'feel' of the stations, thereby reducing crime and fear of crime and increasing patronage.

Dates

The measures were introduced between June and September 1997.

Action

The following measures were introduced:

- a comprehensive CCTV system;
- the stations were completely repainted;
- comprehensive re-signing and improved local information;
- refurbished waiting shelters;
- demolishing redundant station buildings;
- improved fencing to eliminate hidden recesses;
- hanging flower baskets;
- cycle parking facilities;
- murals were painted on a wall previously covered with graffiti.

The total cost of these measures was £96 000. The cost was shared between Connex South Central (£66 000), Railtrack (£10 000) and Lambeth Safer Cities (£20 000).

Outcome

A passengers' survey by Lambeth Public Transport Group, following the completion of works, showed that 14% of men and 24% of women felt safer when using the stations.

Wandsworth Road and Clapham High Street stations had no revenue until ticket machines were installed as part of the project. In the first quarter since installation they showed revenues of £4008 and £2103 respectively. Moreover, passenger numbers have increased so much that Connex South Central plan to lengthen some peak hour trains to cope with the demand.

Case study 18 – Murals at Tooting station (Thameslink)

Objective

To reclaim Tooting station through involvement with and ownership by the youth community. Tooting is on the Wimbledon loop line and is a suburban commuter station.

The project was a joint project with Railtrack and Merton Youth Awareness.

Background

Chronic lack of investment has left Tooting station extremely run down. Although the station has always been well used during the morning and evening peak periods, the general air of neglect created a threatening environment. Public perception of crime meant that customers made minimum use of the service or avoided travelling altogether during off-peak hours.

This encouraged further vandalism and graffiti. The Station Regeneration Scheme provided the opportunity to improve the station, but it was important to ensure that Tooting was also reclaimed for the community. An earlier pilot mural at Morden South in August 1997 was adopted as the model for Tooting station.

A partnership between Railtrack and Merton Youth Awareness Programme (YAP) provided the basis for the funding of materials, design, safety training and equipment, project management and liaison with the graffiti fraternity. Merton's YAP recruited artists for the mural. Participants had to pledge to give up illegal graffiti in order to be eligible to work on the project.

The murals were to be painted onto a series of blank wall panels along both platforms. The walls were primed to create the best possible 'canvas' and to ensure that the finished result would last. Teams of artists worked at night over a weekend in May,

producing their own work. The only proviso was that the finished work should not be offensive to others. Once completed, the differing styles were co-ordinated by a youth worker who layered more artwork on top. The panels were then treated and sealed with anti-graffiti paint.

The murals have been very well received and are respected by other graffiti artists. To date, Tooting station has remained free from vandalism and graffiti. The project has been so successful that a further mural has been commissioned for Mill Hill Broadway.

Benefits

- An attractive colourful environment
- A decrease in graffiti cascading to other stations, both Thameslink and neighbouring train operating companies (TOCs)
- Building relationships in the community
- Increased opportunities for further partnerships for all parties involved
- Positive high-profile publicity and media coverage
- Ownership of the station by the community
- Reduced trespass and vandalism
- Reduced maintenance costs
- Fewer incidents.

Case study 19 – Graffiti removal

Objective

To reduce the incidents of graffiti at Connex South Eastern stations in south-east London.

Dates

1995 to the present.

Background

During the early 1990s graffiti became a serious problem at some stations in south-east London. Connex needed to find a simpler way of protecting its buildings and a quicker method of responding to and removing the graffiti. BTP Crime Prevention Organisation helped Connex to find a company who made a suitable product. The company, Tensid, demonstrated its products and we trialled them. The Tensid system involved applying a non-toxic biodegradable chemical sacrificial coating to surfaces and then removing it with high-pressure hot water cleaning equipment. The hot water system is trailer-mounted, towed around behind a van and has an independent power and water supply. It can be used on any type of surface, porous or non-porous. We decided to buy the product and train staff to use it.

At the same time we set up a central unit to respond to reports of vandalism and graffiti. This unit was supported by a 'hit squad' dedicated to removing graffiti and coating buildings with the new substance. Initially we concentrated on the worst affected route, removing existing graffiti, applying sacrificial barriers and dealing promptly with attacks as they occurred. Once one line was under control, we moved on to the next. Today we can remove graffiti within 24 hours, with a four-hour response for offensive, racist or sexist graffiti.

Outcome

There was significantly less graffiti on the stations. Prompt removal discouraged repetition and helped make the environment less threatening for staff and customers. As a result of our achievements and proven track record, the Station Presentation Team Manager has been elected a founder member of the National Graffiti and Vandalism Association.

Case study 20 – Railtrack Project Vista

Objective

Project Vista was set up to look at the visual impact of line-side management in terms of litter, graffiti, engineering materials and weeds.

The project aims to improve Railtrack's management of operational land, and the way it is perceived. This should result in fewer complaints. The project should demonstrate a genuine business case for tackling these issues in terms of cost savings and cost avoidance.

Background

A paper presented at the Chairman's Meeting on 18 May 1998 responded to concerns raised at the previous month's meeting by proposing measures for short-term, sustainable improvement in the appearance of the rail network. The meeting agreed the following actions:

- Railtrack to gain corporate membership of the Tidy Britain Group (TBG);
- Railtrack to commission a survey of the network covering litter, graffiti and line-side material;
- to set up a pilot project to tackle the problem of line-side tidiness in Scotland;
- to assess the outcome of the pilot before implementing the plan nationally.

Stage 1 of the project will be a survey of the network. Stage 2 will involve using the results of the survey to design an effective pilot project.

Stage 1: survey

TBG to be commissioned to carry out a litter and graffiti survey of the whole network. The results of this survey will be used to identify where contractors are not complying and to set up a system to ensure implementation.

Outcome
Enforcement of existing contract. Recommendations on improved management systems and methodology for continued monitoring to the Contractors' Managers Group (CMG). Development of audit and assessment protocol.

Stage 2: pilot projects

Local knowledge combined with the results of the survey should help identify typical problems. Pilot projects in East Anglia and Scotland Zone will test out methodologies and identify best practice. A high-profile conference will be held in the zones affected to promote the projects.

Outcome
The pilots should identify best practice which the project will then help spread across the zones. The pilots should also enable costings to be sent to CMG.

Project resources

The project will be co-ordinated by the Director of Assurance and Safety with the Southern Zone Environment Manager seconded to the project for between one and two days a week. A full-time assistant will work on the project. A steering group made up of representatives from relevant departments in different zones will maximise the dissemination of contacts and best practice.

Time scales

The project will run for 12 months, after which responsibility will be handed to the Area/General Contracts Manager.

Deliverables

The project will deliver the following:

- a survey report for the whole network covering litter, line-side material and graffiti;

- an internal and external communication network on line-side tidiness which will remain effective at the end of the project;

- an improved perception of Railtrack's line-side management;

- fewer complaints about the appearance of the line side;

- recommendations on best practice in litter management, graffiti management, contractor materials management and weed contract control;

- costed proposals for rolling out the solutions identified in the project across the company.

Case study 21 – Railtrack South Zone fly-tipping investigation

Background

The Environmental Protection Act (EPA) 1990, Pt IV gave local authorities and other statutory undertakers a duty to keep their land clear of litter and refuse, so far as practicable. British Rail was named as a statutory undertaker, and Railtrack Southern agreed to aim for the same standards as laid down in the EPA Code of Practice on Litter and Refuse. It is expected that the duty will be formally transferred to Railtrack by a statutory instrument before the end of 1998.

The EPA Code of Practice on Litter and Refuse sets down the following cleanliness standards:

Grade A – No litter or refuse present

Grade B – Predominantly free of litter and refuse

Grade C – Widespread distribution of litter and refuse with minor accumulations

Grade D – Heavily littered with significant accumulations.

Compliance with the Code of Practice is measured against these graded standards and against set response times, which set time scales for cleaning up. If Railtrack fails to clean an area within the time scales, the local authority can serve Litter Abatement Notices. Failure to comply with these can result in a fine plus a daily fine if the offence continues. Members of the public can also seek Litter Abatement Orders against Railtrack through the magistrates' courts.

Main issues

A recent survey by TBG showed that instances of littering and fly-tipping are fairly evenly spread across the Southern Zone. However, the TBG survey did highlight two areas where fly-tipping is

particularly bad – the Greenwich to Slade Green, and Mortlake to Windsor and Eton lines.

The most common fly-tipped waste was household items such as furniture and mattresses. Black sack bin liners and carrier bags were also common. Fly-tipped waste of a commercial nature, for example builders' rubble, was also noted.

Analysis of the fly-tipping sites shows that fly-tipped waste is most likely to be next to bridges (34%), behind housing areas where housing properties back directly on to Railtrack land (28%) or on Railtrack land (24%). These are the points of easiest access to the railways.

Certain types of fencing seem to encourage fly-tipping. Of the sites we identified, 63% had chain link fencing, 18% had another type (no fencing or fencing other than the main types), 15% had domestic housing property fencing, and only 3% had palisade fencing.

Fly-tipping is on the increase. The Environment Manager identified trouble spots in cities such as Brighton and Southampton and on the Catford Loop, North Kent and West London lines in or around London. It is worth noting that the damage done to chain link fences by fly-tippers encourages further trespass, vandalism and graffiti, and that chain link fencing is much easier to climb or remove with cutters. Replacing chain link with palisade fencing requires a heavy initial outlay but minimises problems in the long term. Reducing fly-tipping also means that fewer vermin are attracted to the sites and that the risk of line-side fires is lessened.

Clearing fly-tipping costs more than £500 per call-out. A recent major clearance at Selhurst cost over £3000. Sixty tons of waste was recently removed from Hassocks.

It costs £45 per metre to install palisade fencing, compared to £18 per metre to install chain link fencing. However, palisade fencing lasts for 25 years compared with 10 years for chain link. Maintenance costs are low, as palisade fencing is very resistant to vandalism. Chain link fencing is very easily damaged and has to be replaced frequently. To prevent fly-tipping, fencing should be 2.4 metres high. For domestic properties, 1.8 metres is acceptable.

At the beginning of 1997, the local authority identified Bromley as a site which suffered badly from fly-tipping. The fence had been broken down and the tipping had spread from Railtrack to local authority land. The maintenance contractor had cleared and replaced the fence on numerous occasions, but the problems remained. The local authority and Railtrack replaced the chain link fencing with palisade. Since then, there has been no fly-tipping on Railtrack land. However, according to the local contracts manager, the local authority are still experiencing problems on their side of the fence.

The options

If no action is taken, the present situation will continue. Action will be reactive rather than proactive. Sites will be cleaned and chain link fencing, with a life span of 10 years, will be replaced as necessary.

Alternatively, the parties involved could take action to identify areas prone to fly-tipping and trespass. Pilot schemes could then compare the cost of clearing and replacing chain link fencing with the cost of installing palisade fencing. Palisade fencing, although more expensive, has an extended life span of 25 years and, as in the case of Bromley, can prove an effective deterrent.

Evaluation and conclusions

It would be too expensive to install the recommended type of palisade fencing throughout the zone. However, the Environment Manager agreed, in conjunction with the Trespass and Vandalism Co-ordinator and local contractors, to install palisade fencing on a trial basis. TBG is willing to monitor pre- and post-installation cleanliness over a specified period of time.

The expense of installing palisade fencing should be outweighed by the savings made in cleaning, maintenance and repair. If palisade fencing proves to be a cost-effective deterrent, it could be set up wherever fly-tipping is a recurring problem.

6 – EDUCATION AND BEHAVIOUR

Education can play an important part in reducing or preventing instances of trespass and vandalism. Educational initiatives such as school visits are important, but so too are others which aim to involve the wider community.

Vandalism: who does it?

The offenders

84 Statistics show that juvenile boys are the most likely offenders and that 'group destruction' is commonplace. However, there are many cases of vandalism where the perpetrator is unknown. From the available data it seems that the incidence of vandalism peaks around the age of 13–15 and then begins to decline. Offenders who have left school tend to have erratic work histories in low status jobs. Research has not shown any links between vandalism and social class or ethnic origin.

Risk factors

85 Research into social delinquency (of which vandalism is one type) identifies a number of social and psychological risk factors. These include poor school achievement, interacting with other anti-social people, a history of childhood aggression or troubles, and anti-establishment attitudes. Possessing a 'sensation-seeking' personality may make someone more likely to become a vandal. Such people seek thrills and adventure and will actively take risks.

86 Certain family factors may also increase the risk of juvenile delinquency. These include poverty (poor housing, large family size), convicted parents or a problem sibling, and parents whose style of child-rearing lacks consistent rules or clear limits.

Protective factors

87 Factors which appear to protect someone from social delinquency include having good social and problem-solving skills, feeling attached to and involved with school, doing well at school and avoiding involvement with anti-social groups around the ages of 12 or 13.

Vandalism: reasons and motivations

88 There is no simple explanation for why people commit malicious vandalism. However, there are a number of theories. These theories assume that there must be some motive, even though the perpetrator appears to gain nothing from the act. Some of the reasons which have been suggested are listed here.

89 *Boredom*. Vandalism may be a reaction to high levels of unemployment and lack of recreational amenities in the community. Indeed, vandals often report that they are bored, and feel the need for action. Vandals have also reported feelings of 'fun and thrills' after committing acts of vandalism both as a consequence of the acts themselves and because of the risk of being caught.

90 *Aesthetic reasons*. Vandalism may be used as a form of artistic expression. This is especially true in the case of graffiti.

91 *Control*. Vandalism can be a way of affecting the environment and therefore feeling some control over it. There are a number of theories about control, including ideas like powerlessness or alienation, learned feelings of helplessness, the perception that someone or something else is in control, competitiveness and self-effectiveness. These ideas tie in with the fact that objects or environments which are vandalised are often regarded as anonymous and that the acts of vandalism often leave a lasting mark on the environment. Researchers note that vandalism is a comparatively safe way of 'making something happen' as the risk of detection is usually low and the physical environment does not hit back.

92 *Behavioural norms*. Groups of individuals have their own standards of 'normal' behaviour, which will depend on factors such as the age and sex of group members and peer pressure. Peer pressure can be an extremely strong influence in younger age groups, particularly among boys. Deterring young people from trespass and vandalism should therefore highlight the need to change peer group thinking.

93 *Perceived risks and benefit*. Groups and individuals have different perceptions of the risks and benefits involved in trespass and vandalism. Research suggests that it is important both to raise awareness of the risks and play down the benefits.

Education

94 This chapter looks at how trespass and vandalism can be prevented through education, media campaigns and community projects. These measures are all linked to the above reasons for vandalism.

95 The public and the media both take a negative attitude to trespass and vandalism on railways. Media reports of fatalities often put the blame on railway managers. Accidents on level crossings tend to be headlined 'Train hits car' even when in fact it was the car that struck the train. Maintaining good relations with local communities and local media can help ensure fairer treatment of railway incidents (see Case study 26).

96 In the 1980s, British Rail's national trespass and vandalism programme focused on school visits. This included provision of a range of support materials and production of *Roald Dahl's Guide to Railway Safety*. A review of the programme in 1993 indicated that it was neither well targeted nor effective. It tended to focus extensively on primary and girls' schools and often visited schools in areas which did not have a problem with trespass and vandalism, or even where there was no railway in the vicinity. BTP evidence showed that most trepass and vandalism incidents were committed by male youths aged 15–19 who often did not attend school. As a consequence, the national programme was abandoned. Railtrack zones took responsibility for providing a more focused and localised programme, concentrating on schools in known problem areas and placing more emphasis on secondary schools.

97 The value of school visits is still debated in the industry and the appropriateness of using uniformed BTP and train drivers is increasingly questioned. South Yorkshire Supertram have been using mature women to carry out their community education programme. This has proved highly successful, and schools may benefit from adopting a similar approach. There has been little structured evaluation of the impact of school visits, although there is evidence that teachers, parents and the general community value school visits which are compatible with the aims of the National Curriculum. See Case study 23 for an illustration. The effect of school visits on children is harder to measure. A thorough review, involving education representatives, parents and school students, would help focus the programme more effectively.

98 Concentrated programmes of short visits, community information and media coverage can be useful when changes are being made to rail services, or a completely new railway operation is about to be introduced (see Case studies 22 and 23).

99 Wider school and community involvement is likely to produce benefits in the long term. Several operators have introduced 'Adopt a Station' schemes involving local schools and communities, and these have proved successful. Case studies 24, 27 and 28 are good examples of effective community involvement.

100 Many local authorities and schools have programmes to promote general child safety, which could be a useful way of getting the message across about trespass and vandalism on the railways.

101 A number of operators, including Railtrack North West and London North Eastern Zones, are using drama projects, the Crucial Crew initiative (see Case study 25), sports programmes and celebrity involvement to spread the message about trespass and vandalism. See Case study 25 for a brief description of these types of events.

102 Initiatives targeting male youths aged 15–19 include Nexus and Connex South Eastern's programme of truancy control (Case studies 30 and 31). There may be scope for extending this initiative in the light of the government's policy on reducing truancy.

103 Nexus's work with detached youth workers could also have wider benefits, given the high incidence of unemployed male youths in trespass and vandalism (see Case study 29).

104 In several areas, efforts have been made to persuade parents to exercise greater control over their children in order to stop them trespassing. Railtrack North West Zone and ScotRail have produced leaflets which they are distributing to houses and at major family events. BTP in the Midlands and Scotland use specially designed road vehicles to take safety messages about the railways into local communities (Case study 32).

105 We understand that the Royal Society for the Prevention of Accidents is also looking at the issue of child trespass in a number of industrial settings, including railways.

Media involvement

106 The media has an important part to play in alerting potential perpetrators, parents and the community in general to the dangers of trespass and vandalism. We can encourage positive coverage by including media personnel in Q-train operations (see section 7), presenting special campaigns to the media and promoting specific events. We cannot expect the media to provide good coverage unless they are fed with fresh stories.

107 Avoiding negative media coverage is also important. Railway public relations managers have a crucial part to play in presenting issues positively.

Youth crime

108 Several organisations are already working to tackle youth crime. The railway industry would benefit from working more closely with them. The Department of the Environment, Transport and the Regions' forthcoming report, *Young People and Crime on Public Transport*, contains case studies which could be helpful for train operators.

Case study 22 – Heathrow Express/British Transport Police/Railtrack

Objective: To reduce or even eliminate incidents on newly electrified lines after the introduction of the Heathrow Express Service by increasing public awareness of this new and potentially dangerous development.

Dates: 1994 – the present.

Background: BTP and Railtrack developed a structured publicity campaign featuring Saracen from TV's *Gladiators*. This campaign took in 155 schools, with each receiving a number of visits.

Outcome: There have been no reported incidents involving overhead line equipment since energisation.

Case study 23 – British Transport Police

Objective: This community initiative aimed to get local people involved in looking after a new line in the Snow Hill area of Birmingham.

Dates: 1994 – the present.

Background: Several initiatives were launched during the construction and initial operation of this prestigious £26 million joint project between Centro and Regional Railways. The initiatives included one focusing on the dangers of trespassing on the line. In another initiative, the three new stations were adopted by two local schools, one junior and one secondary.

Outcome: By involving the local community from the outset and by incorporating crime prevention and safety messages into the curriculum, we maximised awareness of the potential dangers.

Case study 24 – Centro/Regional Railways/British Transport Police

Objective: To reduce incidents of juvenile trespass.

Dates: July 1997 – 3 December 1997.

Background: We identified 'hot spots' and introduced video surveillance. In one location, 70 children from a local school were seen trespassing over a short period.

Outcome: The local school was extremely helpful in identifying offenders. Railtrack North West Zone erected palisade fencing in the area. Some of the children helped to plant a hedgerow in the area, in order to 'plant the seeds of safety'. The local media helped highlight the dangers and bring the initiative to a wider audience.

Case study 25 – Railtrack North Eastern Zone

Awareness campaigns

The zone has introduced a number of awareness campaigns and initiatives in recent years.

I *Dare You*, an educational drama for years six and seven, tackled peer pressure and bullying, with railway crime as a backdrop. Since its premiere in June 1996, 60 000 schoolchildren in the London North East (LNE), North West and Scotland Zones have seen the 45-minute play. A further 20 performances are planned for 1998/99 in the London North East Zone, and the play will also be available in other zones. The play has been welcomed by teachers and educationalists, who believe live drama is an effective way of highlighting key messages. I *Dare You* II, a drama workshop pack, can be used by schools to reinforce the play's themes and safety message in the classroom. As an educational tool I *Dare You* II complies with the National Curriculum's Personal and Social Education module. The unit cost per performance (depending on venue) is around £1200. On average each performance is seen by 350–400 children, with three times that number receiving the core messages through the I *Dare You* II workshop package.

Short Cut is a 10-minute video in soap opera format aimed at highlighting the dangers of using the railway as a short cut. The video also looks at how parents can set an example for their children.

The video has been circulated to every secondary and middle school in mainland Britain (around 5300), where it is being used as part of the personal and social education programme. The total cost, including distribution, is £35 000.

Play it Safe is a 10-minute video in animation format aimed at 5–8-year-olds. The video is based on an original idea by an 18-year-old Sunderland schoolgirl. The characters – Mr Railtrack, PC Transport, Doug the

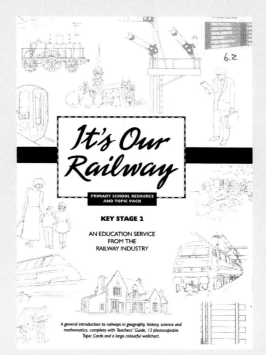

Diesel and Penny the Pacer – help bring key safety messages to life. The video has been circulated to 5000 primary schools in the London North East Zone. A request for funds from HQ to produce enough copies for every primary school in mainland Britain was not taken up. The total cost, including distribution, was £45 000.

Crucial Crews is a 10-minute scenario used in many Railtrack areas. London North East Zone has moved away from a 'model railway' scenario and adopted a more interactive approach. Children step on to a mock up of a railway line and sound effects are used to create the illusion of a train approaching. The scenario is designed to give children a realistic impression of the kind of dangers they face on the railways. It was used in 1997/98 in schools in the southern part of the East Coast Main Line (ECML) Zone and was acclaimed by teachers and safety experts for being realistic and explicit.

A two-week radio advertising campaign highlighting railway dangers ran in the north-east in autumn 1997. Hard-hitting advertisements were backed up by discussion programmes in a fortnight-long campaign. More than 78% of the 600 000 children aged 7–12 who listen to commercial radio in the north-east heard the advertisements at least once. The project cost £20 000.

The zone devised children's colouring books and activity packs incoporating key safety messages. These have been used extensively in the BTP school visits programme as well as at galas and fetes. A board game loosely based on snakes and ladders and reinforcing safety guidelines was also developed.

The zone piloted a scheme in a Leeds school close to a trespass and vandalism blackspot. Pupils were asked to produce their own railway safety newspaper.

In conjunction with BTP we run an annual football tournament for children in inner city areas. Railway safety is the underlying theme and the winners receive the Railsafe Trophy.

Case study 26 – Railtrack North West Zone

Introduction

A spate of tragic incidents on Merseyside's railway network sparked a unique safety campaign by the *Liverpool Echo*, one of the largest circulation evening newspapers in the country.

Railtrack North West Public Affairs were instrumental in launching the campaign and helped the *Echo's* reporting team compile material for the week-long 'Stay Away – Stay Alive' initiative.

Background

Railtrack North West Public Affairs were concerned at the deaths of three youngsters aged 5, 8 and 16 during a three-week period. The department contacted the *Liverpool Echo*, stressing the need to emphasise the 'responsibility factor' when tackling the problem of trespass.

The *Liverpool Echo* then launched a hard hitting week-long campaign that concentrated on the duty of the public (and not just Railtrack) to accept responsibility for the consequences of accidents caused by trespass and vandalism on the railways. In particular, the campaign highlighted the very real dangers youngsters face if they play on or near railways.

The *Echo* began the campaign just two days after the death of an 8-year-old youngster who fell on to the live third rail system used on Merseyside. A few days earlier, a 16-year-old youth had died after allegedly jumping from a bridge on to the overhead line in Liverpool.

Just one day into the campaign, tragedy struck again when a 5-year-old boy was killed after falling on to the third rail in Birkenhead, Merseyside.

This incident gave even greater impetus to the *Echo* campaign. Rather than simply blaming Railtrack for failing to provide adequate fencing, emphasis was placed on the responsibility of the community at large.

The message 'Stay Away – Stay Alive' was hammered home throughout the campaign. Three leader columns were devoted to the subject within a seven-day period.

The cuttings above are from the *Liverpool Echo's* comprehensive campaign. The full-colour three-quarter page graphic that launched the initiative is shown at the start of this chapter. The *Echo* printed 4000 copies of the graphic in poster form and distributed them to schools across Merseyside.

The *Echo* campaign is a unique example of how a positive media initiative can bring railway safety to the attention of the public and encourage them to take responsibility for keeping themselves and children off the railways. The campaign also served to remind Railtrack of its responsibilities for safety and track-side security.

Case study 27 – Connex South Eastern

Background

Aylesham is a colliery town in Kent. Since the colliery shut down, there has been a dramatic increase in unemployment in the town and there is very little for young people to do. The station has become the main meeting place for young people, leading to graffiti attacks and serious vandalism on and around the station.

Project

In July 1996 Connex South Eastern, Kent County Council's Youth and Community Officer and Aylesham Youth and Community Centre met to discuss the situation and to draw up an action plan. The schools' summer holidays had already begun which meant participants needed to move very quickly to make the project successful.

Action plan

The station presentation team painted the platform areas first due to the safety implications, then cleared the vegetation. The Aylesham Youth Project helped with the external and internal painting of the station buildings and fences and cleared rubbish. The Aylesham Youth Project then adopted the station, agreeing to clear litter on a regular basis.

Benefits

- We demonstrated our desire to work with local communities.
- The project improved the look of the station and its surroundings.
- The initiative gave ownership of the station to young people and their community.
- The initiative reduced the number of graffiti attacks and incidents of vandalism at the station.
- We encouraged young people to take an active interest in their environment and local community.
- We showed the community that we care about their environment.
- We demonstrated how much work is involved in station presentation.
- The safety briefing raised awareness of the dangers associated with railways among young people.
- The initiative was a good publicity opportunity for everyone involved.

Outcome

Aylesham was a runner-up in the 1997 Connex South Eastern Smartest Station Competition. There had been almost no vandalism or graffiti at the station since the project began.

Case study 28 – South West Trains/Crime Concern

Objective

To investigate safety issues affecting people using Bracknell station and the Reading line.

Dates

Autumn term 1996 and spring term 1997.

Background

Bracknell and Martins Heron Safer Travel Group invited a Youth Action Group (YAG) to look at safety issues on the Reading to Waterloo line. The Regional Officer of the Youth Action initiative and a Crime Concern consultant worked with Ranelagh School YAG, Bracknell. The students carried out surveys using a questionnaire in school and also canvassed opinion outside, using a press release to invite comments from the public. They also prepared a video diary, made a model of the station and interviewed staff, including the station manager.

Outcome

After four weeks, the YAG presented their findings to the Safer Travel Group and the directors of South West Trains.

- Lighting on the platforms – especially platform 2 – should be improved.

- Staff should be more visible on trains and on the station.

- There should be more signs telling people what is being done to improve safety.

- The appearance of the station should be improved by removing litter and graffiti.

- The public should be made aware of the CCTV system, which could make them feel safer.

The questionnaire results were displayed on graphs and pie charts. Conclusions were drawn based on the original hypotheses.

MPs in the House of Commons invited the group to discuss their findings. The group was also invited to the local police station to discuss youth crime. The group organised a school competition to design a mural to improve the appearance of Bracknell station.

The survey showed that the public felt threatened by groups of young people while they were using public transport. The group prepared a Code of Conduct covering travel to and from school to help pupils understand how their behaviour reflects on their school and how it affects their fellow passengers.

Case study 29 – Nexus/North Tyneside Council

Objective

To reduce trespass and vandalism by young people by using detached youth workers to consult target groups.

Dates
July 1997 – July 1998.

Background

Nexus worked with North Tyneside Council to commission an audit consultation on young people and the Metro. The project was completed in February 1997, and made a number of recommendations.

Since July 1997, Nexus and North Tyneside Council have funded two part-time detached youth workers, who concentrate on a particularly troublesome stretch of railway.

Different initiatives have been launched to encourage youths and the community to 'adopt' the Metro and accept it as integral to their area. Face-to-face sessions led to young people making many constructive suggestions as to how improvements could be made. Support came from parents, members of the local community and other agencies.

We organised special events such as Youth Work Week, which included:

- producing a rap song called *Stand Clear of the Doors*;
- visiting local radio stations;
- producing information packs on various agencies;
- a photography project;
- a quiz competition.

Outcome

The final evaluation is being carried out.

Case study 30 – Truancy control on the Newcastle Metro

Objective: To reduce the number of truants using the Metro system. This would in turn help reduce acts of vandalism and fear among passengers.

Dates: June 1997 to the present.

Background: Four education authorities ran patrols with Metro Police and revenue control staff across the Metro system and in areas surrounding stations. The parents of truanting children were told that their children were missing school. Each 'swoop' lasted one day.

Outcome: On the last day 267 truants were caught, 160 of whom were accompanied by a parent. Altogether 652 children were stopped during the day and three people wanted on warrant were arrested.

Because of the large number of condoned truants (children out of school with their parents' permission), we intend to run a further poster campaign targeted at parents.

Case study 31 – Connex South Eastern/London Borough of Greenwich truancy control

Objective: To reduce the number of young people truanting from school on the rail network, and to reduce the acts of vandalism they cause.

Dates: The pilot ran from 10–21 November 1997. The project is ongoing.

Background: Two truancy officers from the London Borough of Greenwich and one BTP officer ran patrols targeting stations and routes where staff had reported children truanting or causing a nuisance. Patrols worked on stations and trains, stopping children and asking them what they were doing. If they were truanting, teachers and parents were informed. Meanwhile, posters were put up at stations to raise awareness.

Connex staff will get a card with the number of the truancy hot-line so they can notify the truancy patrol if there is a high incidence of truants on the trains in a particular area.

Outcome: During the two-week pilot period the patrols stopped 30 children and young people aged between 9 and 16. Eleven of them had legitimate reasons for being absent from school. However, as the truancy officer noted, 'the 30 children that were stopped will spread the message about truancy patrols on trains'.

The initiative has been successfully repeated, and patrols will now be carried out on a regular basis.

Case study 32 – British Transport Police

BTP liaison vehicle

Following discussions at the bi-monthly trespass and vandalism group, Railtrack Public Affairs decided to finance a vehicle to go into the community and educate the public about the dangers of trespass and vandalism. The initiative was launched in October 1997. The vehicle could also be used for rapid response to major incidents, acting as a post-incident information centre.

The vehicle, which cost £22 500, is a large transit-type van equipped with video equipment which can be used for surveillance or for showing public educational material produced by BTP and Railtrack Midlands. The van also carries information packs for distribution across the community. It seats up to eight younger people, with three police officers in the front.

The van is used in conjunction with the Scarecrow teams by acting as a focal point for the public when Scarecrow has already made its presence felt.

Up to June 1998, the van had made 150 visits to 32 of the 48 high-risk areas within the BTP Midlands area. It attended 11 school fetes and was present at fire and rescue open days in the West and East Midlands. The van was launched with extensive media coverage on 29 December 1997 at Ryecroft, a housing estate close to Walsall which is otherwise known as 'Bomb Alley'.

BURGLARIS DISEMBOWELIS

YOUR FIRST LINE OF DEFENCE

Having been asked by the Essex Police to select a list of plants suitable for their Crime Prevention Initiative, I have spent considerable time and consultation with others to prepare 12 choices which not only have Burglaris Disembowelis properties, but are colourful and fragrant and grow in all soils making them both functional and aesthetic.

Berberis Julianae - Prickly yellow, early flowering species. Evergreen with shiny dark leaves (4-6').

Pyracantha - A climbing Evergreen with yellow, red or orange berries with white flowers in M thorny branches. V useful on fences a walls (10-15').

Mahonia Bealei Winter Sun - Prickly Evergreen with yellow fragrant flowers in Winter (4-5').

Hippaphae Rha Sea Buckthorn any soil and is resistant with foliage and e thorns, this l provides sur Plant in gro obtain berr

Ulex Europaeus - Common Gorse. Viciously Spiny. Flowers March - May (4-5').

Berberis Superba Use this individu Decidu with b foliag in Sp two

Crime
Prevention
Initiative

All plants will be lifted from the nursery bed and immediately packed into stay fresh bags and then dispatched between October and April according to date of order to arrive ready for planting in excellent and fresh condition. In this way plants will be ready for speedy growth as soon as Spring arrives. Instructions for planting and aftercare will be sent with the order. This mode of direct mail order to the Public has been selected in order that the quality of plant material can be monitored at source of despatch

Berberis Stenophylla - Use as a hedge or shrub. Graceful Evergreen with long arching prickly branches, masses of yellow flowers in Spring (4-6'). (allow two plants per one metre).

Rosa Fruhlings Gold - Yellow Fragrant Old Fashioned Rose - densely prickly for hedges or individual shrubs up to 2-3m high.

Berberis Gagnepainii - A small dense prickly evergreen suitable also for a low hedge - impenetrable (allow two plants per one metre).

Rosa Rugosa Rubra - Crimson Fragrant Old Fashioned Rose - densely prickly for hedges or individual shrubs up to 2m high.

Crataegus Monogyna - Common Hawthorn. This forms an impenetrable thorny hedge, attaining only height of your choice. Fast growing, a wonderful sight in May & June with fragrant flower. Red haws in Autumn (Plant in a staggered row 4 to one metre.)

Rosa Blanc Double de Coubert - White Fragrant Old Fashioned Rose - densely prickly for hedges or individual shrubs up to 2m high.

7 – ENFORCEMENT AND DETERRENCE

This section highlights some of the enforcement initiatives which have taken place and the importance of having effective deterrence measures in order to avert trespass and vandalism incidents.

Working with BTP

109 BTP's work in apprehending perpetrators and pursuing appropriate cases through the courts is an effective deterrent. Police crime analysis processes are becoming increasingly effective in identifying priority areas and activities for prevention and apprehension. Working more closely with BTP to deal with railway incidents would improve targeting, prevention and apprehension campaigns.

110 BTP plays an important role in school visits, although the overall value of visits remains open to question. BTP analysis also helps us to select schools for visits.

111 Q-trains, special trains with police officers on board, have proved effective in many areas. Taking media representatives on some of these trips has helped attract positive media coverage. Q-trains can be made more effective by using a road vehicle to shadow the train. This vehicle can then deal with incidents which cannot be tackled from the train. However, this is an expensive way of dealing with trespass and vandalism and needs to be used with discretion (see Case study 33).

112 BTP, Railtrack South and Connex South Eastern have set up line-side patrols in known blackspots and at sensitive times on North Kent suburban lines, using locally based staff (see Case study 34). Railtrack's Operation Scarecrow (see section 4) has also addressed this issue.

113 The police have limited resources. Pooling resources with BTP and other police forces means more patrols, more surveillance and quicker response to incidents.

114 It is crucially important that railway staff, Railtrack, train operators and maintenance/renewal contractors are all involved in observing and reporting activity on the line side. Properly co-ordinated activities can have a major remedial and deterrent effect, especially if staff can be reassured that their reports are being acted upon.

115 BTP in Scotland based their Railwatch scheme on the TV programme *Crimewatch*. The scheme provides volunteers living near the railway with a direct telephone number they can use to report any incidents or suspicious behaviour.

116 Co-operation with Crimestoppers is already reasonably widespread in the industry. However, it could be focused more specifically on the problems of trespass and vandalism.

117 Direct police action to combat disorderly conduct and vandalism at stations can be effective. Case study 35 illustrates this point. Providing feedback for parents was an important part of the initiative, which ties in well with government policies aimed at combating youth disorder.

118 LTS Rail have recently obtained orders banning named individuals from their trains for disorder offences and travelling without tickets. This could also apply to persistent offenders in trespass and vandalism cases. Also, the crime of endangering public safety was used successfully recently by BTP and may be suitable for more extensive use.

Working with the Crown Prosecution Service

119 Much work has been done in the past to help the Crown Prosecution Service and magistrates understand the potential seriousness of the cases presented to them. In a number of cases, defendants have received inadequate sentences because of this lack of understanding. In 1994, Railtrack's Director of Safety and Standards wrote an article in the Magistrates' Association journal *The Magistrate* highlighting the serious implications of trespass and vandalism incidents. HSE, London Underground and train operators have also established contact with the Magistrates' Association.

120 More recently, Railtrack North Eastern Zone produced a slide and video presentation for magistrates' training days. They also approached the Crown Prosecution Service training department about including railway crime issues in their training programmes. However, more work on improving understanding is still needed.

121 Appropriate signs at stations and railway crossings can act as a deterrent. Also, the existence of adequate signs has often been an important factor in magistrates' decisions when considering cases.

122 Finally, the provisions of the Crime and Disorder Act should make it easier to bring successful actions against known vandals and people responsible for other forms of anti-social behaviour. The Act requires local authorities and the police to carry out local crime audits before April 1999 and subsequently to develop and publish a crime and disorder strategy in collaboration with local agencies and partners. It is important that railway industry representatives work to develop these local audits and other strategies to ensure that railway-related vandalism, trespass and other issues are addressed.

Case study 33 – Railtrack/Northern Spirit/British Transport Police

Q-trains

An undercover crackdown on 'Q-trains' has so far caught 51 trespassers and vandals. The anti-trespass and vandalism programme ran throughout the school summer holidays. The programme was organised by Railtrack, train operator Northern Spirit and BTP.

Two further Q-trains will be running in the Newcastle and Leeds areas.

The Q-train is staffed by BTP officers who tour known trespass and vandalism blackspots. Representatives from local media, rail users consultative committees (RUCCs) and industry have been invited to travel on the trains.

Police have uncovered a significant number of incidents, including:

- youths walking down the track with loaded air rifles near Ferryhill station. They also had unleashed dogs with them. The incident took place just a few hundred yards from where a little boy was electrocuted;

- 6-, 8- and 9-year-olds placing railway ballast and concrete troughing on the line just outside Goole station;

- a 10-year-old found playing on tracks in the Hull area was found to be 'blind drunk';

- teenagers swinging from trees above the running lines near Billingham;

- two children and their parents were playing with motorbikes on the line at Aldwarke.

Most of the other trespassers were taking a short cut.

We intend to work closely with other businesses to tackle the problem of trespassing and reduce the number of incidents.

BTP is collating all incidents and will put each case to the Crown Prosecution Service. BTP will ask the CPS to look closely at all incidents and, where possible, to prosecute. A report will be published when the Q-train initiative is over.

Media coverage

Yorkshire Evening Post, Leeds
Yorkshire Post, Leeds
BBC Look North news programme
YTV's Calendar news programme
Tyne Tees TV
Radio Aire FM
BBC Radio Cleveland
BBC Radio Humberside
Goole Courier
Goole Times & Chronicle
Railnews
Sheffield Star
Halifax Evening Courier
Middlesbrough Evening Gazette
Darlington & Stockton Times
The Northern Echo
Evening Chronicle, Newcastle
Rotherham Advertiser

Some representatives of the West Yorkshire media travelled more than once on the Q-trains. At the end of the project all media will receive a press release with all the incidents listed and a fact file from BTP listing the number of trespassing and stone-throwing incidents.

Case study 34 – Connex South Eastern/Railtrack South/British Transport Police

Objective: To prevent trespass onto the railway and stone throwing from line side and station areas in the south-east London area (all lines from Dartford to London) during the school summer holiday.

Dates: July and August 1997.

Background: School-age children are responsible for a large number of incidents involving trespass and vandalism. This is a particular problem during the school summer holidays. A team from Railtrack, BTP and Connex South Eastern patrolled the area every day during the holiday. All team members were local and therefore aware of the main blackspots.

The team had a remit to talk to children about the consequences of their actions. Where necessary, BTP followed this up with parents. The team also had to respond to incidents reported by staff, identify more permanent remedial measures to prevent trespass and vandalism such as bridge caging, and generally act to deter delinquent behaviour.

Outcome

- Two adults were arrested and formally cautioned by the police.

- Six adults received warning letters from the police.

- Police visited and warned the parents of 27 juveniles.

- 150 juveniles were spoken to at the scene and given guidance and warnings about trespass.

Case study 35 – British Transport Police

Objective: To prevent youths consuming alcohol and drugs and acting in a disorderly fashion from frequenting stations in the Manchester area.

Dates: 1996/97.

Background: Disorderly groups of youths were gathering in stations in the Manchester area. The police had taken action, arresting or reporting offenders. The parents of youths who had not committed any crimes received letters warning them about their children's behaviour and presence at the stations.

Outcome: The arrests and reports reduced the problem. The operation was replicated in other areas.

8 – CONCLUSION

What are the key points arising from this publication? Two of them are undoubtedly the need for partnership in addressing this problem and the evaluation of all trespass and vandalism-related activities.

123 This publication has highlighted many of the factors which cause or influence acts of trespass and vandalism, and many of the ways in which the railway industry is trying to combat them. If you or your railway company are affected by trespass and vandalism, we hope this publication has helped you to understand the problem and to consider some appropriate responses.

124 First, it is important to appreciate that the railway is an integral part of the wider local community, and is affected by its problems. It is therefore important to consider approaching agencies and organisations outside the railway industry to help formulate a joint response to the problem. Working in partnership with all interested agencies is crucial. Multi-agency working and co-ordination of activities can also help.

125 The next step is to develop a policy statement on tackling trespass and vandalism and to link it to your existing environmental policy statement.

126 When planning your policy statement, it may help to consider the following points:

- *What* are the particular problems you face?

- *What* information and evidence do you have?

- *How* can the problems best be tackled and *what* action do you think is appropriate ?

- *When* will any action start and *who* will carry it out?

127 The next stage is implementation: putting the measures/actions you have decided on into practice.

128 Once the strategy is in place, it is important to monitor its effectiveness. You can evaluate this by considering the following questions:

■ *Has* the action been successful?

■ *Has* it had the desired effect?

■ *How* is the action seen by others?

■ *What* lessons can be learnt?

129 Combating trespass and vandalism is an ongoing process, not a one-off exercise or campaign. Careful planning, taking action, monitoring its effectiveness and evaluating what you have done will help you develop effective responses to the problems caused by trespass and vandalism both now and in the future.

FURTHER INFORMATION

Publications

Secure Stations Scheme: Guidelines for Operators (1998, DETR). Available from Mobility Unit, DETR, Zone 1/11, Great Minster House, 76 Marsham Street, London SW1P 4DR.

Preventing Vandalism: What Works? (1994, ISBN 1 8589 3298 X). Available from Home Office Police Department.

Risks to the Public at Unsupervised Stations (1997, HSE Contract Research Report). Available from HSE Books, PO Box 1999, Sudbury, Suffolk CO10 6FS. Tel: 01787 881165.

Railtrack Trespass and Vandalism Research and Strategy Study (1998, Railtrack). Available from Railtrack Safety & Standards Directorate, Railtrack House, Euston Square, London NW1 2EE.

It is our Railway (Railtrack Primary Schools Pack). Available from Railtrack Southern Zone, Suite 2, Floor 2, Waterloo Station, London SE1 8SW.

Supporting a Friendly Environment (SAFE) – A Strategy for Safe Travel on Public Transport in South Yorkshire. Available from South Yorkshire Passenger Transport Executive, PO Box 801, Sheffield S2 5YT.

Safe School Trips – A Safety Code for Users and Suppliers of School Transport (Scottish School Board Association). Available from Scottish School Board Association, Newall Terrace, Dumfries DG1 1LW.

Roald Dahl's Guide to Railway Safety (British Railways Board).

Videos

Short Cut, a 10-minute video highlighting the dangers of using railways as a short cut (1995, Railtrack). Available from Railtrack London North Eastern, Public Affairs, Main Headquarters, Station Rise, York YO1 1HT. Tel: 01904 524943.

I Used to be a Vandal, a training video (1995, Railtrack). Available from Railtrack. Tel: 01793 499097.

Play it Safe, an animated video about the dangers of playing near the railway (1996, Railtrack). Available from Railtrack, Public Affairs, Main Headquarters, Station Rise, York YO1 1HT. Tel: 01904 524943.

Note: The future availability and accuracy of the references listed in this publication cannot be guaranteed.

Organisations for further information

The following organisations are members of the RIAC Prevention of Trespass and Vandalism Working Group. Please contact them if you wish to get further information.

Railtrack

Main HQ
Station Rise
York YO1 1HT

Tel: 01904 524943
Fax: 01904 523698

London Transport

50–64 Broadway
London SW1H 0DB

Tel: 0171 222 5600

Crime Concern
Signal Point
Swindon
Wiltshire SN1 1FE

Tel: 01793 514596
Fax: 01793 514654

British Transport Police
PO Box 260
15 Tavistock Place
London WC1H 9SJ

Tel: 0171 830 8883
Fax: 0171 383 5315

Freightliner Ltd
CP 404
Tower Block
1 Eversholt Street
London NW1 2FL

Tel: 0171 383 0750

Connex South Eastern
Room 20, First Floor Offices
Cannon Street Station
Dowgate Hill
London EC4N 6AP

Tel: 0171 234 1179

South Yorkshire Supertram
11 Arundel Gate
Sheffield S1 2PN

Tel: 0114 275 9888

**Transport Salaried Staff's Association
(trade union)**
10 Melton Street
London NW1 2EJ

Tel: 0171 387 2101
Fax: 0171 383 0656

Central Rail Users Consultative Committee
Clements House
14–18 Gresham Street
London EC2V 7NL

Tel: 0171 505 9090

Nexus
Metro Control Centre
Station Road
South Gosforth
Newcastle upon Tyne NE3 1PZ

Tel: 0191 203 3333
Fax: 0191 203 3181

Railway Industry Advisory Committee
Secretariat
5 SW
Rose Court
2 Southwark Bridge
London SE1 9HS

Tel: 0171 717 6322
Fax: 0171 717 6670

INDEX

Printed and published in the UK by the Health and Safety Executive C25 12/98